LIVING
EMBLEMS

Ancient
Symbols
of
Faith

Restoration Foundation

Understanding the Jewish roots of our faith is a golden key that unlocks the treasures of Holy Scripture and enriches our Christian lives. This fundamental concept is the focus of Restoration Foundation, an international, transdenominational, multicultural publishing and educational resource to the body of Christ.

Restoration Foundation features scholars, church leaders, and laypersons who share the vision for restoring the Hebrew foundations of Christian faith and returning the church to a biblical relationship of loving support for the international Jewish community and the nation of Israel.

We are pleased to make available to all denominations and fellowships the teaching of the gifted scholars and Christian leaders. Conferences and seminars are available on a wide range of topics.

We publish *Restore!* magazine, a high-quality journal featuring theological balance and scholarly documentation, that helps Christians recover their Hebrew heritage while strengthening their faith in Jesus.

Restoration Foundation also distributes Golden Key Books in order to disseminate teaching about Christianity's Judaic foundations.

The ministry of Restoration Foundation is made possible by our many partners around the world who share in our Golden Key Partnership program. We invite you to join us in sharing the satisfaction of knowing that you are a partner in an organization that is making a difference in the world by restoring Christians to their biblical Hebrew heritage, by eradicating Judaeophobia and anti-Semitism, by supporting Israel and the international Jewish community, and by encouraging collaborative efforts among those who share this vision.

For information about Restoration Foundation, *Restore!* magazine, Golden Key Books, and Golden Key Partnerships, contact us at the address below.

Restoration Foundation
P. O. Box 421218
Atlanta, Georgia 30342, U.S.A.
www.RestorationFoundation.org

LIVING EMBLEMS

Ancient Symbols

of Faith

John D. Garr

GOLDEN KEY PRESS

Restoration Foundation
P. O. Box 421218
Atlanta, Georgia 30342, U.S.A.

To our sons,
David, Tim, and Steve,
who gave Pat and me great
joy as youngsters, made us
proud with their academic
accomplishments, and now
stand solidly with us as
men, sharing with us the
joy of God's
blessings.

TABLE OF CONTENTS

Preface

For centuries Christian theologians have searched for a theological sarcophagus for Judaism, the religion their theories have purported to be a lifeless, fossilized system. With the advent of Christianity, they have asserted, Judaism became a superfluous anachronism, serving only as a monument to the futility of man's works and standing in marked contrast to the efficacy of Christian faith. Like the ashes of yesterday's fire, Judaism deserved to be buried and forgotten. Along with the demise of Judaism, the Jews themselves were to have faded into history with little more than a faint remembrance of the quaint, obstinate people who had been cursed for their obduracy and their rejection of Jesus.

From Marcion, the heretic of the early second century, until equally heretical theologians of the present, Christians have sought to establish the idea that Jesus destroyed Judaism. And if they could not confirm Jesus as the terminator of Judaism, then at least Paul, the apostle of justification by faith, was the "pathologist" of Judaism, whose autopsy of that dead religion found it to be an eviscerated, empty shell, totally lacking in vital substance, overwhelmed by pandemic legalism and self-righteousness.

The serious and inexplicable problem for this Christian postulation is that, despite all their theological pronouncements and the predicted and hoped-for demise of

Judaism and the Jewish people, *Am Yisrael Chai!* (the people of Israel live!). Defying all the laws of history for the assimilation of conquered and vanquished peoples, Jews have continued to exist as an identifiable entity, the greatest living testimony to the existence of an immutable God (Malachi 3:6). And Judaism has continued to be a vibrant faith, ever drawing the Jewish people into loving devotion to their God. Not cooperating with the Christian agenda of history, Jews have held tenaciously to their faith in spite of overt, systematic, and unrelenting persecution from a triumphalistic church and political systems that bore the name *Christian*.

Nothing could illustrate this truth more eloquently than the various biblical emblems that represent Judaism and the Jewish people. To most Christian theologians and leaders, these are lifeless relics of a failed religion, but to Jews and to a growing number of Christians who are reclaiming the Jewish roots of their Christian faith, these ancient symbols are living emblems. They attest to a living faith in the God of Abraham, Isaac, and Jacob, a faith that came to include all Christians when one of Israel's own sons, the Jew from Nazareth, brought God's light to the nations through the agency of his reformed congregation (the church).

"Don't even begin to think that I have come to destroy the Torah [law] or the prophets," Jesus declared. "Not even one *yod* [the smallest Hebrew letter] or one tittle [the crowns or decorative strokes of the Torah text] will ever fail until all is fulfilled," he affirmed (Matthew 5:18). Jesus came only to imbue new life into God's ancient, miraculously validated faith, restoring it to its original intent and purposes. As Martin Buber, one of the greatest Jewish thinkers of our time, has declared, the earliest Palestinian Jesus movement was a radical call to doing Torah. Every aspect of biblical Judaism and much of Second Temple

Judaism's tradition were affirmed in Jesus' teaching. This included the various God-given symbols for Jews that subsequently became important for Gentiles as the faith of Israel became the faith for all nations. Because of Jesus, the living emblems of Judaism became vibrant symbols for Christians, not only renewing memories of the Hebraic foundations of the Christian faith that were manifest in the lives of Israel's patriarchs, but also pointing to eternal life through the person and work of Jesus Christ.

Unfortunately, millions of Christians have been denied the enriching understanding of these ancient emblems of the divine faith. The riches of their rightful heritage have been replaced with the baubles of Gentile tradition, relics from ancient Babylonian polytheism and paganism. Priceless heirlooms of spiritual insight have been quietly replaced with the costume jewelry of "Christian" tradition. The riches of Judaism that the apostles made available to the Gentiles when Israel's leaders did not accept Jesus as Messiah have been replaced by Hellenic philosophy and Latin political systems.

"Enough!" is the outcry of millions of Christians around the world. "We've been robbed!" they are protesting. A fresh summons to return to the God of the Bible and to the People of the Book is echoing across the landscape of Christianity. Believers of every faith communion are diligently engaged in recovering the church's lost legacy in Judaism and among the Jewish people. Christian arrogance and boasting against the natural branches of God's family tree of salvation are being challenged by men and women of faith and humility for whom *truth* is far more important than *tradition*. The time has come for a full restoration of the ancient faith of the earliest fathers of Christianity, including those of the first covenant.

The living emblems of Judaism are attracting Christians like a spiritual magnet, even though many Christians who are so exercised have little idea why they are suddenly drawn to things Jewish. It is the Holy Spirit that is bringing restoration to the Christian community by quickening in Christian hearts this connection with Jews and Judaism. Since the emblems of Judaism were birthed from the heart of God's people, Israel, and were manifest in God's Word, it is only natural that the Holy Spirit should quicken in God's new covenant people an attraction to such things. After all, the job description of the Holy Spirit is, in the words of Jesus, to "guide . . . into all truth" (John 16:13).

For traditional Jewish people, the emblems of Judaism are vibrant reminders of their special election as covenant partners with God. They are calls to remembrance and renewal that ever fulfill their designed function of maintaining the Jewish people under the guardianship of the Torah. As signposts, they point the way to God and to divine truths that have been essential to Jewish faith for centuries. These symbols are alive with meaning, full of depth and significance. As milestones and semaphores, they carefully mark the path of *halakhah*, the Jewish way to walk in faithful obedience to God and his Word.

For Christians, biblical emblems are living portraits of Jesus as Messiah and Lord of the church. Jesus himself declared that all that was manifest in the covenant under which he had been born was a material witness validating his person and work (John 5:36, 39). Paul and other apostles affirmed the ongoing validity of objects and observances of the first covenant as propaedeutic of Jesus, adumbrating the reality that was manifest in his life and ministry (Colossians 2:17; Hebrews 10:1). For Christians, then, Jewish symbols are still living emblems, pointing the way to the one Life who fully revealed all of God's will manifest in the Torah and thereby established the perfect righteousness that is imputed to the believer for his faith.

Christians may borrow and adopt Jewish emblems with their historic, traditional symbolism in a mature, responsible mind set. They must be careful, however, that drawing Christological conclusions from these symbols not become artificial and incongruous, a kind of emblematic supersessionism, as it were. Christian applications must be seen as complementing Jewish understandings of their own emblems, not as a co-opting of them that could rightly be seen as a defiling desecration, a mocking expropriation of *sacramenta*.

We must follow the example of Paul who honored his fellow Jews as having profound advantages, affirming that to them were committed the very Word, glory, covenants, and service of God (Romans 3:1-4; 9:4-6). At the same time Paul recognized Jesus as the fulfillment of Israel's Messianic expectations, declaring unequivocally that "Christ our Passover is sacrificed for us" (1 Corinthians 5:7). The apostle's teaching neither abandoned the tradition of his ancestors nor replaced it with a new "church" tradition. Instead, Paul maintained his rich Jewish heritage through his belief in all things written in the law and the prophets (Acts 24:14). Central to his understanding of the continuing Jewish heritage, however, was his conviction that all of the Hebrew Scriptures foreshadowed the coming Messiah, whom he recognized as Jesus of Nazareth.

In this book, we will discuss the various outward symbols of the Jewish faith and their continuing importance both to Christian understanding of the life and work of Jesus and to the worship experiences of the church. We will chronicle the historical development of these emblems from their design and first implementation through their use in biblical Judaism and Second Temple Judaism, including the sect of Judaism that came to be called Christianity, into their manifestations in the two millennia of subsequent rabbinic Judaism. We will suggest ways in which Christians can interrelate with their Jewish brothers and sisters in recognizing these living emblems and employing them in honorable, spiritual ways. We will also caution against misuse and abuse of this part of our heritage from the Jewish people in the economy of God's salvation. As naturalized citizens in the commonwealth of the Israel of God, we share in the entitlements of this ancient faith; however, we must do so with dignity and honor, respecting the sensibilities both of those who brought us this rich legacy and of their physical descendants. We believe you will be enlightened and enriched as you share these insights.

I wish to express my personal thanks to my friends and colleagues in the quest to enlighten the church about the Hebrew foundations of Christian faith, Dr. Charles and LuEllen Bryant-Abraham, for their invaluable input of ideas and assistance with the manuscript. I am also indebted to Judy Grehan and Rev. Sandy Clark for their tireless efforts in helping to ensure the quality of the finished product. I am also grateful to my friend Zvi Zachor for his encouragement and help in the design and production of this book. Then, I am thankful to my many colleagues around the world who have shared insights concerning Christianity's Jewish roots that have contributed to this volume.

Shalom & Blessings!

John D. Garr, Ph.D., Th.D.
Pentecost, 2007

Chapter 1

Vital
Signs

Signs along the roads we travel can often mean life or death. If we observe the warnings, go in the prescribed direction, and maintain the proper speed, we find ourselves safe, even in the most dangerous of situations. Life is just the same. We hurtle along through a short, fast-paced existence that is often very unforgiving. We are constantly at risk to the dangers both of our own minds and the actions of others that militate against our success. We are tempted by our own desires and by the devices of *haSatan* (the trap setter) to nurture thoughts and engage in activities that can destroy us mentally, spiritually, socially, and physically. That is why we need the biblical signposts that point us toward life, creating in us the character and actions that are strong vital signs.

A LIVING FAITH IN THE LIVING WORD

The faith of what the church has almost pejoratively called the "Old Testament" is not a jejune, lifeless religion that should long ago have been buried in the sands of time along with other failed systems. The People of the Book are not legalists who should have been assimilated into the nations where they were dispersed, never to be remembered again. Both the people and the Book are chosen of God and are manifestations of his immutability (Malachi 3:6) and of his irrevocable covenants (Romans 11:29). God cannot lie

(Hebrews 6:18), and he cannot change (Hebrews 13:8). If Judaism were ever his system of religion for mankind, in some form it must remain so. And so it is. Biblical Judaism produced many Judaisms at the beginning of the Common Era; however, only two have survived, Rabbinic Judaism and Christianity–sister religions, as it were. All that is authentic in religious experience today is firmly rooted in the biblical Judaism through which the prophets and sages of Israel and Jesus and the apostles of the church expressed their devotion to God.

The Word of God is both the Hebrew Scriptures (including the Apostolic Writings) and the Incarnate *Logos* (John 1:14). The "Old Testament" is the Bible that Jesus and the apostles used to preach the gospel of the kingdom (Luke 24:44; Acts 24:14; 2 Peter 1:19). It is the "God-breathed" Scripture that is profitable for teaching and instruction in righteousness so that believers may be mature and equipped for every good work (2 Timothy 3:16). That is why it is so vital for the church to "search the Scriptures" (John 5:39), because what the Hebrew prophets, kings, and sages wrote as they were carried along by the Holy Spirit (2 Peter 1:21) is that which testifies of Jesus and Christian faith, validating both for all time as the fullest expression of devotion to God.

It is not enough, however, to be hearers and believers of the Word of God: we must be doers also (James 1:22). For far too long, the Christian church has been characterized by dogmatic faith, championing belief but failing to practice what it preaches. It has focused on orthodoxy when God is more concerned with orthopraxy. Jesus affirmed that what would cause the church to be the light of the world would be its "good works" (Matthew 5:16), not just its faith or its doctrinal beliefs, be they ever so sublime. The world will immediately recognize his disciples, taking note of those who have "been with Jesus" (Acts 4:13) when it sees the manifestation of transcendent love that is shed abroad in the believers' hearts by the Holy Spirit, a love that completely fulfills all the Torah (Romans 13:10) by imitating the life of Jesus in good works extended to "the least of his brethren."

The Word of God is not a static, exhaustible resource. It is a living Word that brings renewal and fresh insight each time we examine it. This truth is succinctly stated in Hebrews 4:12: "The Word of God is alive and powerful." By design, everything that is recorded in the pages of the Bible points us to faith in the Messiah. The panorama of events, characters, and material objects manifest by God among his chosen people contained symbols, similes, metaphors, allegories, types, and shadows of events, characters, and spiritual matters that were to be manifest in the life of Christ and the church (Colossians 2:17; Hebrews 10:1).

The truth of this principle in no way diminishes the importance of what God did in pre-Christian times, nor does it minimize the value of what he continues to do with and among his chosen Jewish people even to this day. This understanding does provide a foundation that validates the authenticity of what he has chosen to do among the Gentiles through the One who brought Israel's light to the nations (Isaiah 42:6; Acts 26:23). Jesus is the new and living Way who *filled* the law and prophets *full*, adding depth and meaning to their predictions by demonstrating what the Word made flesh would mean to the entire world: full and free salvation by grace through faith. He completed the faith of his Heavenly Father and of his earthly ancestors, validating that faith's authenticity by providing an efficacious sacrifice and imbuing its renewed covenant with eternal life.

CALLS TO WORSHIP

The many material objects that God either designed himself or that his people constructed as manifestations of their obedience to his Word are living emblems, material symbols that take on life and meaning because of what they reveal. "The invisible things of God from the foundation of the earth are clearly seen, being understood by the things that are made . . . so that men are without excuse" (Romans 1:20). Though God is never *worshipped* through or in material objects, he is, nevertheless, *revealed* through what he and men have made. Just as the universe bears witness to the existence and nature of its Maker, leaving men with no excuse for failing to seek, find, and obey the Eternal God, so the material objects that God instructed his people to fashion are semaphores that call man to remembrance. These sacred symbols ever point the way to God, serving as guideposts that escort man past the treacherous precipices of life into the safety of life-giving relationship with his Maker.

While our feeble attempts to fulfill the Divine will do not always hit the mark and more often than not are flawed, the continued effort is what is important. Anyone who approaches God in simple faith he will never be rejected (John 6:37). When we seek to do his will, he accepts the best we have to offer and gently leads us toward the more perfect day (Hebrews 6:1; 1 Corinthians 12:31). Visible symbols of faith and remembrance bring us to the more excellent way of pure and total love that is manifested both towards God and towards man, thereby fulfilling the requirements of God's commandments (Galatians 5:14).

For the Jewish people, the *tallit*, the *mezuzah*, the *tefillin*, and other objects they have fashioned in fulfillment of God's commandments are signposts along the road of faith that mark the way in which they should walk (*halakhah*). They are constant, visual reminders that they are God's chosen people and that their chosenness makes them servants to him and to the world. They are living emblems that bespeak the life and vitality of God's Word and his covenants with his people.

It is no coincidence that the Talmud combined the commandments regarding *tzitzit*, *mezuzah*, and *tefillin* into a single tripartite unit. These became the insignia of a practicing Jew: "Whosoever has the *tefillin* on his head, the *tefillin* on his arm, the *tzitzit* on his garment, and the *mezuzah* on his doorpost is secure against the commission of sin . . . Beloved is Israel, for the Holy One, blessed be he, surrounded it with *mitzvot*. *Tefillin* on the head, *tefillin* on the arm, *tzitzit* on the garment, and *mezuzot* on the doorposts" (*Menachot* 43b). These three *mitzvot* were considered linked by the three sections of the *Shema*, the great commandment: "Hear, O Israel, the Lord our God is one Lord."

We Christians can also profit from these and other biblical emblems, recognizing them as authentic expressions of devotion to God and his commandments, as well as objects that have fulfilled their avowed purpose in pointing the way to God and to interaction with him. They lead us Christians to Christ, revealing in their dynamic symbolism the meaning and depth of Christian faith, bringing richness and fulfillment to our lives. That which God has ordained works!

Rather than being attractions to sideline us in routine, repetitious ritual, the material objects that God has inspired men to make from his written Word jog our memories and point us unfailingly to the living Word. We celebrate not the objects themselves, but the Lord who is manifest in and through the principles that they reveal. The mature believer uses the object or symbol as a reminder, an aid to concentration on the invisible reality that the emblem represents.

Sensory Perceptions

We must remember that we are attuned to sensory perception that was created by God himself. We are impacted by what we see, hear, smell, touch, and taste. Our faith, therefore, is not some sublime mental exercise or even an attempt to detach ourselves from both mind and body in an effort to contact the "god within," as monists do. Our faith is a living faith that involves every aspect of our being–body, soul, and spirit. We worship God with all our heart, soul, mind, and strength (Mark 12:30). Even our meditation is both a mental and a physical exercise of repeating with our lips the very Word of God (the meaning of the word *meditate* in Psalm 1:2).

When we interact with God, therefore, it is not just through subliminal meditation. We understand God through the visible symbols that he has commanded, or that we have devised, to literalize our interaction with him. We see God in visible symbols. We hear God in music and the spoken Word. We taste God in the Eucharist and in the table fellowship of the Christian meal that is shared with believers in any setting. We smell God in the rich aroma of the fruit of the vine, in the pungent anointing oil, in the incense, in the smoke of candles. We touch God when we hold his Word in our hands, when we physically embrace "the least of his brethren."

Emblems, then, are alive and powerful for us, for through them we materialize the Word of God, transposing it from the abstraction of faith into the reality of good works that glorify our Father in heaven. Just as love is not love until it proceeds from the abstraction of a substantive to the action of a verb, so faith is not faith until its germ seed is brought to full flower in good works (James 2:20, 26).

GUIDEPOSTS, MILE MARKERS

Emblems should ever be billboards that grab our attention in the maddening pace of the modern world, shouting, "Stop!", "Remember your Creator," "Make time for

God." We rush headlong, often down precipitous paths, striving to fulfill our ambitions, seeking the satisfaction of self actualization. We need someone to ring the bell, flash the lights, and drop the barricade to stop our mad rush toward a self-fulfillment that excludes God and our loved ones. God is that Someone, and the bells, lights, and barricades that he has erected are those symbols, emblems, and markers in time that he has specified in his Word.

For Jews, the various outward material symbols of their faith are daily reminders that they are utterly dependent upon God's grace and mercy. Every time they pass through the door of their homes and touch the *mezuzah* that contains God's Word they are reminded that *El Shaddai* is their protector. Each time they bind *tefillin* on their arms and on their foreheads, they recognize that God's commandments are to be written in their hearts and in their minds. Every time they wear a *tallit*, they recognize that their very existence is enveloped in God's commandments.

We have strong evidence that Jesus himself, as a Torah-observant Jew, used each of these mnemonic devices. He was without sin, so necessarily he kept all the Torah's commandments, including these. Archaeologists have discovered *tefillin* contemporary with Jesus' generation, proving that they were then in use in much the same form as the Rebbe Tam *tefillin* of today. Likewise, one of the earliest relics ever discovered in Israel is an inscription on hammered metal which likely held the contents of a home *mezuzah*.

What rich lessons the emblems of Judaism teach us Christians! We have the uniform of the Holy Spirit enshrouding us with God's Word. Because the New Covenant has engraved God's Torah on our hearts and in our minds by the Holy Spirit, we can easily identify and feel comfortable with the outward visible symbols of Israel's ancient faith. We understand that what was literalist and material for the Jews was also emblematic of spiritual realities that dominated their lives and maintained their fellowship with God. We realize that we can share in these elements of our Hebraic heritage because they underscore the most important realities in our lives–the person and work of Jesus as Messiah and Lord and the impartation of the Holy Spirit, which empowers us to fulfill the Word of God in works of faith. And because we have the living Christ within, we are well on our way toward being living emblems ourselves, living "epistles" written and read of all men (2 Corinthians 3:2), witnesses to the saving grace of God through the good news of our risen Lord.

The Shofar

Perhaps the oldest of all biblical symbols, the shofar is mentioned over eighty times in Holy Scripture. Across the past four millennia, the wailing, penetrating blast of the shofar has summoned millions of believers in God to prayer, repentance, and renewal. Its distinctive sound has been associated with Jews and Judaism because every Jew is commanded to hear the voice of the shofar, the trumpet blast that calls Jewish believers from the mundane and focuses their attention on the Divine.

THE AKEDAH

Each time the piercing sound of the ram's horn falls upon Jewish ears, it brings vividly to mind that their faith rests upon the faithfulness of Abraham, the first Hebrew, to hear and obey the voice of God. The binding of Isaac (the *Akedah*) is foundational to Judaism (and to Christianity, for that matter), for through this act the patriarch Abraham confirmed his lifelong devotion to the God who had chosen him and called him to enter the Promised Land in search of the foundational city whose architect is God (Hebrews 11:10). This was God's final test for his friend, who had first heard God's voice calling him out of Babylon into the Promised Land. A Babylonian by birth, a Syrian (Aramean) by nationality, and an idol maker by trade, Abraham was as purely Gentile as it is possible to be. He became the first Hebrew, however, when he responded to the clear, shofar-like blast of God's voice to abandon his idolatry, to embrace monotheism, and to leave his own land for the land that would become Israel.

Because of Abraham's demonstration of radical, unequivocal faith in offering his beloved son Isaac, the ancient patriarch received from God's own hand the substitutionary sacrifice that would stand forever as a symbol of vicarious atonement, the bringing of men into relationship with God through the death of another. The ram that was substituted for Isaac in the burnt offering on Mount Moriah was held firmly in the grip of divine providence by the horns of his head that were crowned in a thorn bush. The horns that were yielded in quiet lamb-like submission to divine sacrifice became the source of the clarion call to community, to repentance, and to faith.

All of the subsequent sacrificial system of the Torah was grounded upon the binding of Isaac, which was seen in ancient Judaism as a vicarious atonement for all of Abraham's subsequent posterity who imitated his faith by obeying God's commandments. The *Akedah* demonstrated God's *chesed*, his tender mercy toward his people, his justifying them solely on the merit of their confidence in his loving kindness.

To this day, the *Akedah* is intrinsically involved in *Rosh HaShanah*, which begins the ten days of introspection that conclude in Judaism's highest and holiest day, *Yom Kippur* (the Day of Atonement). The story of the binding of Isaac in the Torah reading for the second day of *Rosh HaShanah* reminds Jews everywhere that their faith rests on the faithfulness of Abraham's obedience to God. When the shofar sounds, the sonic symbol portrays the ram caught in the thicket that was substituted for Isaac.

GOD SOUNDS THE SHOFAR

According to ancient *aggadot* (Jewish folkloric legends based on the biblical text), God himself blew the shofar at Mount Sinai four centuries after the *Akedah*. That profound blast was a summons demanding the presence of his chosen people at his mountain to become a nation of priests and his witnesses to the entire world. The sages of Israel have observed that when God's voice thundered forth the Ten Words (the Decalogue), all the peoples of the earth heard the words of the fiery law in their own languages. God's shofar blast that had summoned Israel to Sinai also awakened all the nations of the earth to hear the summation of his divine will for mankind: five commandments delineating man's relationship with his Creator and five commandments outlining man's relationship with his fellow man. The cloven tongues of fire that made the Ten Words visible to Israel also resounded into the world, offering God's commandments to the nations. To a degree, these commands were impressed on the consciousness of all mankind so that the Gentiles who have not the law are a law unto themselves, with their consciences either excusing them or accusing them (Romans 2:14-15).

Only Israel, however, responded to God's Law: "All that the Lord has said, we will do, and we will hear [intelligently]" (Exodus 24:7, author's translation). This is the eternal truth about hearing the shofar blast as well as the rest of God's commandments. They are ineffable. It is only through experiencing them, through doing them, that one understands them. Israel manifested the only right reaction to God's commands. With Abrahamic faith, Israel responded immediately and unequivocally to the divine initiative. "Whatever you say, we will do; and then we will understand." When one *hears* the shofar, he *understands* the summons of the divine voice that has echoed across the corridors of history, bringing God's chosen people into intimate relationship with their Father and King (*Avinu, Malkenu*).

The penetrating, soul-stirring sound of the shofar is a call to separation. It is an incisive voice as if from heaven, calling the hearer to withdraw from the routine of life into the presence of the Almighty. Since the very first biblical reference to the shofar is at the Sinai theophany, this living emblem constantly summons those who hear God's voice to "come out from among them and be separate" (2 Corinthians 6:17). The Hebrew word *shofar* derives from the Hebrew root *shafar*, which means to shine as with a brilliancy of sound. It is so called because it makes a clear and sharp sound, hinting at a brilliant burning into the heart of God's purposes. It is an incisive call of separation, a demarcation between the world of the profane and the Divine. The Hebrew root also indicates beauty. Perhaps its call to separation is a part of God's summons of his people to the "beauty of holiness" (1 Chronicles 16:29; Psalm 96:9).

For forty centuries, then, the ram's horn has been the trumpet that has called God's people to repentance, faith, and devotion. In ancient times, it was also used as a means of alerting the people to danger and for calling them to assembly and to war (Judges 3:27). It was used as an accompaniment to other musical instruments (Psalm 98:6), in processionals (Joshua 6:4ff), as a signal (Joshua 6:16ff; 2 Samuel 15:10), and as a means of instilling fear (Amos

3:6). To this day, it is used at various times of significance and solemnity among Jews, including the inauguration of political leaders to public office. It is the shofar that produces the distinctive sound so readily associated with the Jewish people around the world and in the nation of Israel.

A SHOFAR FESTIVAL

The shofar is the central element in one of Judaism's major holy days, *Rosh HaShanah*, the Jewish civil new year. (*Rosh HaShanah* literally means "head of the year.") This day signals the beginning of the most solemn time of the year for observant Jews, the Ten Days of Awe, which conclude in the Day of Atonement, Judaism's highest and holiest day. The shofar heralds to the Jewish people: "Stop! Stop to reflect on your own mortality, and stop to confront your personal morality." It is a blast that demands to be heard, a material sound that commands, "*Shema*" ("Hear" or "Listen, and obey"). The repeated blast of the shofar fulfills one of its most important functions, that of summoning Israel to repentance (Hosea 8:1). Its rousing, wailing sound echoes through gatherings of the Jewish people for the Day of Trumpets, when the shofar is sounded one hundred times to ensure the fact that it is blown often enough and with proper sounds to satisfy God's requirements and to alert the Jewish mind to the significance of the Day of Atonement.

For thirty days prior to this day throughout the month of *Elul* (except the first day, the last day, and each *Shabbat*), the shofar is sounded daily, urging Jews to examine their conduct and their relationships with God and man. Along with the Ten Days of Awe between *Rosh HaShanah* and *Yom Kippur*, this makes a total of forty days of introspection for Israel, parallel with the time of probation allocated for Nineveh in ancient times (Jonah 3:4) and the forty years of Israel's probation in the wilderness.

On the first day of the month *Tishri*, however, a great celebration of the blowing of *shofarot* (shofars) ensues. As a matter of fact, this festival day is also called *Yom Teru'ah*, the day of blowing, blasting, or shouting. In Jewish tradition, this day is the anniversary of the creation of the world, when the voice of God in a shout like the sound of a shofar brought forth the universe out of nothing. It is particularly apropos that, on the anniversary of creation, believers should be summoned to recognize the sovereignty of God and to be in awe of the Almighty.

In the ten days that follow *Rosh HaShanah*, the shofar is blown on each weekday as a summons to soul-searching and repentance. Finally, its blast is heard most solemnly at the conclusion of the Day of Atonement (*Yom Kippur*), signaling the end of this day of fasting, intense introspection, and repentance.

On *Rosh HaShanah*, Psalm 47 is recited seven times before the sounding of the shofar, reminiscent of the Israelites' seven circuits around Jericho before the walls fell. It is also symbolic of the seven heavens through which prayers must penetrate to reach the throne of God. Central to this Davidic passage is the proclamation in verse 5: "*Alah Elohim b'teru'ah*; *Adonai b'kol shofar*" (literally, "God ascends with the blasting; the Lord with the sound of the shofar"). The sounding of the shofar indicates the enthroning of God in the hearts of those who hear the sound.

The shofar sounding on *Rosh HaShanah* features, first, the broken notes that resemble sobbing, the *teru'ah* sound (consisting of three medium blasts in succession), then the notes that resemble wailing, the *shevarim* sound (consisting of nine short, staccato blasts), and finally the long unbroken blast called the *teki'ah gedolah* (great blast). The *teru'ah* (including the *shevarim*) resembles the sobbing, wailing, repentant petitioner, while the *teki'ah* represents the blast that enthrones the King. The enthroning of God as King must always outweigh the sobbing repentance, for it is only through the grace and mercy of the Eternal that the penitent is forgiven and given life. Jewish tradition insists that the *teki'ah* must be of greater length than the *teru'ah*. The *teki'ah gedolah* is held as long as the trumpeter can hold the note (often more than one minute).

The shofar is blown during the *Musaf* (additional) service on *Rosh HaShanah*, the first series (thirty blasts) before the *Amidah*. The second series (thirty blasts) is blown during the repetition of the *Musaf* and integrated into the narratives describing God's kingship, the Jewish forefathers' merit, and the hopes for the Messianic Age. Timing for the remaining blasts varies according to tradition among various Jewish communities.

A Time Alarm

God thought it important to set apart specific *mo'edim* (appointments) on his calendar, times for meeting with his people. He also provided an alarm to summon them to those appointments. The alarm that made a certain, distinct sound was the shofar. It was unmistakable, a clarion call to worship the King enthroned in the hearts of his people.

The shofar was blown at the temple to begin the Sabbath. Two men with silver trumpets and one man with a shofar sounded three blasts twice during the day. It was blown to signal the beginning of the festivals (Numbers 10:10), to confirm the time of the new moon each month (Psalm 81:3), and to summon the solemn assembly (Numbers 10:2; Joel 2:15). The shofar also accompanied various instruments in temple music (Psalm 98:6; 150:3-6). Since the temple does not exist today, the use of silver trumpets is virtually unknown; however, the Yemenite shofar is still used at the Western Wall in Jerusalem to announce the onset of *Shabbat* and the festivals.

The sounding of the shofar occurred on occasions when people stood solemnly before God and declared the truth. The making of oaths was often accompanied by the shofar's sound (2 Chronicles 15:14). The distinct sound, harking back to God's covenant and oath with Abraham, solemnized such events.

A REPENTANCE SYMBOL

The shofar is a symbol of both power and repentance, and even of the power of repentance. The sounding of the shofar insists that Jews be prepared like Abraham to sacrifice all for their faith in God. It also recalls that God has made provision for atonement of sins for the truly penitent heart. Repentance that begins in earnest with the blast of the shofar on *Rosh HaShanah* prepares the way for forgiveness on *Yom Kippur*.

While it was originally used to assemble the people and to prepare and direct warfare, the shofar came to be a penitence symbol in the time when King Asa proclaimed a new covenant: "Seek the Lord, the God of their fathers, with all their heart and all their soul . . . with trumpets and *shofarot*" (2 Chronicles 15:12, 14). Some scholars declare that the shofar itself is a symbol of repentance. Its curved shape exhibits the head that is bowed and the heart that is bent before God. Its sound mirrors the desperate sinner's cry for mercy from God. At the very least, however, it is a shocking, stark reminder that halts life's feverish pace, clearing the mind and heart for introspection so that even hidden sins may be recognized and dealt with in true repentance (Psalm 139:23-24).

The Jewish idea of repentance is manifest in the Hebrew word *teshuvah*, which means "to turn." It is through recognition, remorse, return, and resolution that one is fully repentant. First, one must recognize his sin as an offense

against God and/or his fellow man, an act that produces
the Godly sorrow or remorse that is essential to repentance (2 Corinthians 7:10). Then, he must turn from and
renounce that sin. Finally, he must resolve that when presented with the same temptation, he will not succumb to
it again. In this action, the penitent hears in his heart the
shofar blast and reacts to the divine initiative that restores
relationship both with God and man.

In the sixth century before the Common Era, Zechariah introduced a new meaning to the sound of the shofar–that of salvation: "And the Lord shall be seen over
them, and his arrow shall go forth as the lightning: and the
Lord God shall blow the trumpet [shofar], and shall go
with whirlwinds of the south." The shofar is the herald of
salvation, God's deliverance of his people. Centuries after
Zechariah's time, the expectation of salvation was still
manifest in Judah Maccabee's ordering his warriors to blow
shofarot, not to frighten the enemy, as was the case with
Gideon, but to invoke God's assistance and salvation.

THE SOUNDS OF THE SHOFAR

The harp and the shofar are the most mentioned musical instruments in the Bible. The harp was used to soothe
the spirit (cf. David's skillful playing that calmed the evil
influence in Saul) and to console hearts troubled by life's
vicissitudes. The shofar, on the other hand, was used to
seize the attention of God's people and prepare them for
whatever cause his purposes demanded.

There are various kinds of shofarot, taken from sheep,
goats, antelopes, and gazelles. The Talmud declares that a
shofar should preferably be of a ram's or a wild goat's horn
(because they are curved). Only the horn of a cow is for-
bidden for use as a shofar because it is a reminder of the
golden calf incident at Sinai. A shofar may be gilded or
carved, provided that the mouthpiece remains natural; how-

ever, it may not be painted.

The large spiraled horn that is the most common symbol of Jewish prayer is the Yemenite shofar, the horn of the Kodo, an African antelope. Yemenites prefer this horn because of the scriptural injunction that a "big shofar" be sounded and because of its deep bass notes. The *Sephardim* (Jews of Spanish and Portuguese extraction) favor this shofar because of its low and ceremonial tone. The *Ashkenazim* (Jews from German and Eastern European backgrounds) prefer a smaller shofar, one made from a sheep or goat horn that produces a higher, more shrill, supplicating sound.

The various tones of the shofar are determined by six factors: 1) the size of the drilled hole; 2) the proportion between the top and bottom of the mouthpiece (a larger proportion makes the best sound); 3) the thickness of the bone; 4) the diameter of the mouthpiece (which should be proportional to the size of one's mouth); 5) the texture of the horn; and 6) the size and length of the shofar. A shofar of the best quality will produce at least three notes; others may produce only one or two. An accomplished *ba'al hateki'ah* (master of the sounding) can perform amazing musical feats with the instrument, producing as many as seven notes!

The Bible refers to two kinds of shofar sounds: *teki'ah* and *teru'ah* (Numbers 10:5-8). The *Mishnah*, however, prescribes three sets of shofar sounds since the word *teru'ah* is mentioned in the Bible three times (Leviticus 23:24; 25:9; Numbers 29:1). It identifies the *teki'ah* as a long blast and the *teru'ah* as three wavering, crying blasts. The *teki'ah* (blowing) is a glissando, beginning on a low note and swelling to a higher note. The *teru'ah* is a series of staccato blasts on the lower note. The *shevarim* is an alternation of higher and lower notes, a tremolo of nine staccato blasts. The blowing of the shofar is in three sets of sounds: first, *teki'ah, shevarim–teru'ah, teki'ah*; then, *teki'ah, shevarim, teki'ah*; and finally *teki'ah, teru'ah, teki'ah*. The sounding is concluded with a *teki'ah gedolah* (great blast), a note that is drawn out for as long as the trumpeter can hold it, signifying that the Divine Presence (*Shekhinah*) went into exile with Israel and rests upon a quorum (*minyan*) in prayer.

In Jewish tradition, the shofar is generally sounded only in the daytime; however, at the end of *Yom Kippur*, after the *Ne'ilah* service, the shofar is blown again well after nightfall. The shofar is also sounded in the Sephardic *selichoth* (penitential) services which begin well before dawn on each weekday from the second of Elul until the day before Sukkot.

A Command to Hear

Fortunately for many Jewish people, God's commandment is for "hearing" the shofar blast, not for the "blowing" of the shofar. Proper sounding of the shofar is somewhat difficult. If the requirement were for "blowing" the shofar, every person would have to perform this act; however, one who is qualified may blow the shofar so that all may hear the blast of the ram's horn, thereby fulfilling this commandment.

Before blowing the shofar, the *ba'al hateki'ah* recites the following benedictions as the congregation responds with "Amen": "Blessed are You, O Lord our God, King of the universe, who sanctified us with your commandments, commanding us to hear the sound of the shofar. Blessed are you, O Lord our God, King of the universe, who granted us life, who sustained us, and who enabled us to reach this day."

During the prayers of the day, ten biblical texts which speak of God as King are recited, along with ten texts which underscore the fact that God remembers and ten texts which speak of the shofar. Ten texts are chosen because the world was created with ten words and is sustained by ten words (ten commandments).

In this way, tradition says that God tells his people: "Recite before me on *Rosh HaShanah malkhuyyot* [kingship], *zikhronot* [remembrance], and *shofarot*: *Malkhuyyot* so that you may proclaim me King over you; *zikhronot* so that your remembrance may rise favorably before me; and through what? Through the shofar."

REASONS FOR SOUNDING

Sa'adiah Gaon, the great Talmudic scholar and leader of Babylonian Jewry, offered the following ten reasons for sounding the shofar:

1) to proclaim the sovereignty of God (because the shofar is sounded at a coronation, and God is proclaimed as King).

2) to herald the beginning of the ten days of repentance.

3) as a reminder to be faithful to the teachings of the Torah, since the shofar blast accompanied the giving of the Torah at Sinai.

4) as a reminder of the prophets, the teachers of righteousness, who raised their voices like the shofar to touch the conscience of the nation.

5) to the sound of trumpets the temple fell, and to the sound of trumpets it will be restored.

6) as a reminder of the *Akedah*, since the ram that substituted for Isaac was caught in the thicket by its horns.

7) to inspire awe as Amos 3:6 declares: "Shall the shofar be blown in a city, and the people not tremble?"

8) as a summons to the heavenly court on the Day of Judgment to be judged, for the prophet Zephaniah calls the great "day of the Lord" (judgment day) a "day of shofar and alarm" (Zephaniah 1:16).

9) as a reminder that the shofar will call together Israel's scattered remnants to return to the Holy Land, for

Isaiah 27:13 speaks of the great shofar which will herald the Messianic Age.

10) as a reminder of the day of resurrection, for the shofar will be sounded at the resurrection.

The thirteenth century Sephardic Talmudist and philosopher, Maimonides, gave this poignant description of the shofar's sound: "Awake O sleepers from your sleep, O slumberers arouse ye from your slumbers, and examine your deeds, return in repentance and remember your Creator."

SHOFAR AND TRIUMPH

Because the shofar is made from the horn of a ram, it is also a symbol of power. Throughout the Scriptures, horns have been used to demonstrate political or military authority (cf. the two-horned ram and the single-horned goat of Daniel 7). The shofar was used in Israel as a means of assembling armies and directing warfare. It was used both to bolster the confidence of the Israelite military and to strike fear in the hearts of enemy contingents. It was believed that the sound of shofar would confuse the evil powers in the heavenlies, even frightening them away from the camp of Israel. While the shofar was used in every Israelite conflict, two of the greatest military accomplishments in Israel's history featured the sound of the shofar.

The first of these were the week-long marches circumscribing Jericho, the impregnable walled city that first confronted the upstart Israelites in their quest to conquer the Promised Land. In an unusual military strategy, seven priests led the parade encircling the walls that concluded in seven circuits on the seventh day. When the *shofarot* blasted the message of God's victory, the walls of Jericho fell down flat before the armies of Israel (Joshua 6:5). This is a clear lesson that no battlement constructed by man or Satan can stand before the presence of God's voice of victory.

The second most prominent use of the shofar in military action occurred when Gideon led a pitifully-outnumbered contingent of only three hundred men against an overwhelming hostile force. Each man was given a shofar, along with a pitcher and a lamp hidden inside and was ordered to surround the enemy force encamped in the valley. When the signal was given, the warriors sounded their *shofarot* and broke their pitchers, exposing the lamps (Judges 7:16-18). The confused enemy thought it was being ambushed by an overwhelming force because it was the custom for large military contingents to be headed by a leader blowing a shofar and carrying a lamp. In the confusion that resulted, the enemy was completely routed by the minuscule force that had the faith to employ God's strategy by going out to battle with lamps and trumpets. This is a clear lesson to those who believe God to win the battle with the sound of his voice.

A still future engagement, the climactic battle of the ages, will be fought by the Lamb with seven horns (Revelation 5:6). Armageddon will be won when the Word of God that proceeds from the Messiah's mouth destroys the enemy force (2 Thessalonians 2:8; Revelation 19:15). The power symbolized by the seven horns will subdue all the armies that have gathered themselves against Jerusalem and the people of God and will usher in the everlasting dominion of the Messianic Age.

THE TRUMPET IN ZION: CHRISTIAN EXPRESSIONS

The prophecy of Joel 2 concludes with the announcement that God will pour out his Spirit upon all flesh in the last times. Peter claimed this prophetic pronouncement for the church and specifically for the profound event that occurred on the day of Pentecost following the ascension of Jesus when the Christian believers were "filled with the Holy

Spirit." This prophecy begins, however, with these solemn words: "Blow the trumpet [shofar] in Zion" (Joel 2:1).

The earliest Christian believers were this prophetic Zion, part of the core of Judaic faith in that day. Later, Gentiles were grafted onto God's family tree of salvation (Romans 11:24) and covenantal relationship to become "fellow citizens" with the saints in the commonwealth of Israel (Ephesians 2:11-13). Since all Christian believers are, spiritually speaking, a part of Zion, it is appropriate that the same trumpet that is sounded in Israel be heard in the church.

David made a universal declaration when he enjoined the praise of God with the sound of the shofar (Psalm 150:3; 98:6). Those Christian believers who are reclaiming the Jewish roots of their faith will recognize in the shofar's sound the call to righteousness and holiness. The shofar, therefore, may be used in the ritual of Christian worship and as an instrument in musical performances.

The shofar should be treated with honor and respect as a venerable instrument set apart to God's service, not as a toy or a means of drawing attention to oneself. One should remember the binding of Isaac as an idea foundational to Christian faith's vicarious atonement. One should also be reminded of the fact that throughout history thousands of Jews have given their lives in sanctification of the name of God rather than submit to pagan rituals or concepts. Like the ram that was slaughtered so that the shofar might sound, so the martyrs of history, both Jews and Christians, have given their lives as a clarion call to true discipleship.

THE GREAT SHOFAR

The tenth of the eighteen benedictions in the *Amidah*, a prayer that is recited daily in synagogues around the world, petitions God for the blowing of the Great Shofar that will signal the coming of the Messiah and the ensuing age of peace. The expectation among the Jewish people is that the Great Shofar will be sounded again at the end of days as it was at Mount Sinai. This expectation is confirmed by Zechariah 9:13-16's prophecy: "I will rouse your sons, O Zion, against your sons, O Greece, and make you like a warrior's sword. . . . The Sovereign Lord will sound the trumpet [shofar]; he will march in the storms of the south, and the Lord Almighty will shield them." This is the time for the sounding of the Great Trumpet at the coronation of the Messiah, described in Isaiah 27:13: "And in that day a great trumpet [shofar] will sound." This is the reason that the shofar has been blown in Israel at the coronation of kings and is still blown at the inauguration of presidents. "And they blew the shofar, and all the people said, Long live King Solomon" (I Kings 1:39).The blowing of the shofar, therefore, signals a change in the political order.

Interestingly enough, the Jewish Apostolic Writings (New Testament) predict that the return of Jesus as Messiah and Lord will be accompanied by the sounding of the shofar. Though the writings themselves use the word *trumpet*, the implication is clear. These were Jewish men writing about the coming of the Jewish Messiah, and they were underscoring the fact that his appearance would be accompanied in grand Jewish tradition, with the blasts of *shofarot*.

The Apocalypse even predicts that seven *shofarot* will sound immediately prior to the coming of Jesus. Each of these *shofarot* has a message in its sound. The first six will be harbingers of wrath to the inhabitants of the earth. The seventh shofar will declare: "The kingdoms of this world are become the kingdoms of our Lord, and of his Christ; and he shall reign for ever and ever" (Revelation 11:15). The fullness of the kingdom of God will be announced by the sound of the Great Shofar, which will assign all earthly dominions to the sovereignty of the Jewish Messiah.

In keeping with his tradition as a Pharisee, Paul predicted the resurrection and the coming of the Messiah and declared that both would be accompanied with the sound of the shofar: "In a moment, in the twinkling of an eye, at the last trump: for the trumpet [shofar] shall sound, and the dead shall be raised incorruptible, and we shall be changed" (1 Corinthians 15:52). Paul's use of the term *last trump* confirms his understanding of the ancient concept of three trumpet blasts: the first trump (at Sinai), the last trump (at the resurrection), and the great trump (the enthroning of King Messiah). At the first trumpet, Israel was married to God, and at the last trumpet, the church will become the bride of Christ.

In 1 Thessalonians 4:16, Paul underscored this longstanding Jewish tradition that the Messiah will come with the sound of the shofar: "For the Lord himself shall descend from heaven with a shout [*teru'ah*], with the voice of the archangel, and with the trump [shofar] of God: and the dead in Christ shall rise first." Paul's statement is in continuity with Jewish tradition which connects the resurrection with the sound of the shofar. Isaiah 26:19 declares of the resurrection, "Awake and sing, *ye that dwell in the dust*." This passage parallels Isaiah 18:3: "All ye inhabitants of the world, and *ye dwellers on the earth* . . . when the shofar is blown, hear ye." The sages teach that the "dwellers on the earth" are those that "dwell in the dust," the righteous dead.

Just as the shofar blast has always served as a call to assembly, so it will be the summons to assemble the resurrection. All things, both in heaven and on earth, will be assembled into one (Ephesians 1:10) with the resurrection of the dead and the gathering of the living (Matthew 24:31; 2 Thessalonians 2:1; 1 Thessalonians 4:16).

Paul was not drawing on some pagan ceremony of eastern mystery religions, predicting the blasting of brass horns to signal the initiation of a Gentile kingdom on earth.

He was applying his extensive rabbinic training to the understanding that had come to him by divine revelation: Jesus is Messiah and Lord, and he will return as promised to establish God's dominion over all the earth. The announcement of that great event will be an earth-shaking blast of the Great Shofar, the "last trumpet." (Paul calls the Great Shofar "the last trump" because it is the last of the seven *shofarot* that will be sounded at the transition from the kingdoms of men to the kingdom of God. In this instance, he combines rabbinic tradition's last trump and great trump.)

GOD'S TRUMPET

From the beginning of God's covenantal relationship with Abraham until the consummation of the covenant in the Messianic Age, the ram's horn is a key element as a symbol of repentance and vicarious atonement. It has always served as a blast of awakening, summoning God's people to introspection, repentance, and renewal of their covenant with God. It has been a material indication of God's manifest presence (Exodus 19:16). It has also been a call to assembly (Jeremiah 4:5) and to war (Nehemiah 4:19-20). Christians can profit from such a reminder of the foundation of the faith of Abraham, completed in Jesus, and of its ultimate consummation in the kingdom of God.

Chapter 3

The Menorah

The menorah has the distinction of being the only emblem in either Jewish or Christian worship and tradition that was designed by God himself. All other emblems represent man's response to God's call, symbols that recall or memorialize great events of history or serve as material objects needed to fulfill divine imperatives (e.g., the *mezuzah* fulfills in literal terms the commandment to write the Torah on the door posts of one's house, while the *tallit* [prayer shawl] fulfills the commandment to append fringes to the corners of one's garment).

The seven-branched candlestick, however, was of divine design, with a heavenly manifestation that likely first appeared when God's Word created the heavens and the earth. Though it was a significant implement in the tabernacle and temples, the menorah has become more motif than apparatus.

THE HEAVENLY BLUEPRINT

In Exodus 25, the Eternal gave specific instructions to Moses, detailing the design of the menorah. When the comprehensive blueprint was completed, the prophet was commanded to "make all things according to the pattern shown to thee in the Mount" (Exodus 25:40; Hebrews 8:5). Apparently Moses was permitted to peer into the heavenlies and there to see the divine pattern for praise, worship, and service, the system employed by the heavenly hosts themselves from the time of creation. Hebrews 8:5 speaks of this event: ". . . who serve unto the example and shadow of heavenly things, as Moses was admonished of God when he was about to make the tabernacle: for, See, saith he, that thou make all things according to the pattern shewed to thee in the mount." The seven-branched lampstand was one of the objects that Moses viewed, one of the living emblems of heaven itself that is of profound significance to those on earth who approach the Creator in worship.

Centuries later, John, the disciple whom Jesus loved, had a similar experience on the Isle of Patmos, a moving account of which is chronicled in the Revelation. First, the apostle viewed a spectacular manifestation of the resurrected Messiah standing in the midst of seven golden candlesticks (Revelation 1:12, 13). When John subsequently viewed heaven itself, he observed seven flames of fire burning before the throne of God. John was told that these seven lamps were the "seven spirits of God" (Revelation 4:5) and that these "seven spirits" are "sent forth into all the earth" (Revelation 5:6).

The heavenly throne was, no doubt, the source of Moses' inspiration, the pattern according to which he was to build everything in the tent of meeting in general, but specifically the menorah. (The altar of incense was also patterned after the "golden altar" in heaven on which, according to John, the prayers of the saints are offered by the angelic host [Revelation 5:8; 8:3, 4]. The ark of the covenant with its mercy seat and two covering cherubim was patterned after the throne of the Almighty.)

The design for the menorah was given in much detail in Exodus 25:31-40; 37:17-24. The lampstand that was to be the only light in the tabernacle was not to be a composite of several pieces joined together. It was to be carved of one solid piece of gold, "one beaten work," and it was the only appliance in the tabernacle that was to be of "pure gold" (Exodus 25:36). The menorah was to have seven lamps of fire atop seven branches that stemmed from one central shaft. The branches were to be richly embellished with almond blossoms formed like cups and with other decorations, including knops that were likely shaped like almonds. The flowers of the uppermost cups on each branch served as receptacles for the seven lamps.

The term *candlestick* used in some English translations is a misnomer, for the menorah was not a candle holder. Rather it featured oil lamps with wicks in the tradition of the ancient means of providing light. Probably the original menorah had bowls of oil atop its branches with a floating wick in each bowl. Later versions probably featured a channel through which the oil in the bowls was drawn to the wick. This would have allowed for the positioning of the lights in different directions.

There has been much speculation as to the actual appearance of the menorah. Traditionally, it has been viewed as having three curved semicircular branches on both sides of a central shaft or lampstand. Each branch rose to the same level as the central shaft. This view is reinforced by the bas-relief on the Arch of Titus, which depicts the menorah among the various spoils from the temple which the Roman general brought to Rome following his conquest of Jerusalem. It is ironic that this design of the menorah memorialized as part of the booty of a conquered Israel is today employed on the official seal of the restored State of Israel. The semicircular design for the branches of the menorah is reinforced by many archaeological discoveries dating to pre-Christian times.

Various Jewish sages, most notably Maimonides, have suggested, however, that the menorah was comprised of a central shaft from both sides of which three straight branches emerged at acute angles to the shaft to reach the same height as the central lampstand. In his commentary on the Torah (*Terumah 25:32*), Rashi, the great eleventh century Jewish commentator, explicitly writes that the branches "extended upward in a diagonal." Indeed, the very Hebrew word used to describe the branches, *kinim*, implies a straight line. Maimonides' son, Rabeinu Avraham, in his commentary to *Terumah*, noted that "the six branches ... extended upward from the center shaft of the menorah in a straight line, as depicted by my father, and not in a semicircle as depicted by others."

Based on the carved reliefs on the Arch of Titus, it has been asserted that the menorah rested on a two-tiered hexagonal base. On the other hand, there is both archaeological evidence and rabbinic commentary to suggest that the base may have been triangular, shaped more like a tripod. The sages have suggested that the menorah had feet extending from its base, which would serve to support the tripod base theory (*Menachot* 28b). Others have suggested that both depictions may be correct, with the two-tiered hexagonal base added to the tripod to give additional support.

Whatever the case may have been, there is no doubt that there was a lampstand in the tabernacle that featured seven branches with seven lamps and that this was the only light of the sanctuary. And, interestingly enough, the menorah is the only sacred symbol that has never been polluted or used for purposes of the pagan or occult.

ISRAEL, GOD'S LIGHT TO THE NATIONS

When God chose the Jewish people, he established them to be a reflection of his light to the nations of the world. The Talmud encapsulates this concept in these words: "Israel said before God: 'Lord of the Universe, thou commandest us to illumine before thee. Art thou not Light of the world, and with whom light dwelleth?'–'Not that I require your light,' was the divine reply, 'but that you may perpetuate the light which I conferred on you as an example to the nations of the world!' "

The Jewish people have long viewed the menorah as symbolic of their calling to be a light unto the nations (Isaiah 42:6). The sages emphasized the fact that light is not a violent force; Israel is to accomplish its mission by setting an example, not by using force (Zechariah 4:1-6). They also taught that the menorah is a "testimony to all the inhabitants of the world that the Divine Presence rests within Israel." The purpose of the menorah was not just to illuminate the sanctuary, but to spread its light throughout the entire world. This idea is underscored by the traditional design of the windows of the sanctuary which were narrow on the inside of the wall and wide on the outside of the wall, indicating clearly that the light of the sanctuary would expand outward.

Since light was God's prime creation, man, who was formed in God's image, was intended to dispel darkness. It is for this reason that the menorah's lamps have spoken to Jewish believers for centuries of enlightenment, learning, understanding, and reason. And this light has not been restricted to an elite few with esoteric knowledge. It has been made the province of all men. Because light is seen as producing joy and happiness, the Jewish people's worship services have never been characterized as somber or ominous.

Israel's commission is to demonstrate to the nations that success is not achieved nor victories won by physical strength or military might. The light of the menorah symbolizes the spiritual illumination of a life inspired by insight from the Divine, a life that is consequently filled with meaning and substance. As the Psalmist declared, ". . . in thy light we see light" (Psalm 36:9).

Isaiah 60:1, 3 predicted that Israel will arise and shine and that "the Gentiles shall come to thy light." Isaiah 42:6 also declared, "I the Lord have called thee in righteousness, and will hold thine hand, and will keep thee, and give thee for a covenant of the people, for a light of the Gentiles." The prophecy of Isaiah 49:6 is also applicable to Israel: "And he said, It is a light thing that thou shouldest be my servant to raise up the tribes of Jacob, and to restore the preserved of Israel: I will also give thee for a light to the Gentiles, that thou mayest be my salvation unto the end of the earth."

Simeon declared Isaiah's prophecy would be fulfilled in Jesus (Luke 2:32). It was the Rabbi from Nazareth, who, through the agency of his congregation (the church), brought Israel's light to the nations, thereby fulfilling God's commission to his ancestors. And he still employed Israel's metaphor: "Ye are the light of the world," a likely allusion to the menorah, for he implored his *talmidim* (disciples) to put the light on a "lampstand." This statement from the Sermon on the Mount was made around the time of the Festival of Tabernacles when the huge temple *menorot* were burning so brightly that all of Jerusalem was illuminated and when there was dancing in the streets of Jerusalem celebrating the majesty of the Eternal. The historical context of this statement also gives clarity to Jesus' other metaphor for his congregation: "A city situated on a hill cannot be hid," for there was no concealing the city situated on Mount Zion, Jerusalem the Golden.

GOD'S LAMP–MAN'S LIGHT

Because of the fact that the menorah has been so closely identified with the Jewish people–and, indeed, has come to symbolize the nation of Israel–it has often been called the "Jewish" candlestick. Believing it to be a symbol of an antiquated religion, most Christian teachers have seen little significance in the menorah for the church and have cast it with nonchalance into obscurity. But, is the appellative *Jewish menorah* wholly accurate?

The truth is that the menorah is God's lamp, a fact that is clearly set forth in 1 Samuel 3:1-3: *"the lamp of God* . . . in the temple of the Lord, where the ark of God was . . ." The menorah is not merely the Jewish candlestick or the tabernacle lampstand or the temple candelabrum. If a title is needed, it is "God's lamp."

In that the menorah is God's lamp, it belongs to all of God's people, both Jews and Christians. Its rich symbolism is appropriate to both faith communities. It represents the bringing of God's light into the world, the light that lightens every man. Since it was the only source of illumination in the tabernacle, the menorah represents the power of vision and insight that comes to believers in God, both Jew and Gentile, by means of God's Word.

It was no coincidence, then, that David called God's Word "a lamp to my feet, and a light unto my path" (Psalm 119:105). This Hebrew word for "lamp" in David's observation is *ner*, the term used specifically for the menorah in Exodus 27:20 and 1 Samuel 3:1-3. That this lamp symbolizes the Word of God is further confirmed in Proverbs 6:23 where Solomon declared that the commandments (Hebrew: *mitzvot*) are a lamp (*ner*). It is likely that the "lamp" to which David and Solomon referred was the menorah, God's lamp and man's light.

Assuring as the light of a torch in an unfamiliar pathway on a moonless night, the Word of God gives vision and direction, illuminating the narrow pathway that leads to the gate of eternal life (Matthew 7:14). Without clear insight into the Word of God, people perish because they cast off restraint (Proverbs 29:18). When illumination from God's Word is not manifest, people lack vision, and when insight is not present, people slide down the slippery slope of deception and plunge often irrecoverably off the precipice of heresy. Because the Word of God is not predominant in their hearts, humans wantonly and profligately throw themselves into the vortex of unrestrained passion and as result reap the judgments of their lack of insight and devotion to the things of God. On the other hand, happy are they who keep God's commandments (Proverbs 29:18).

The Word of God is like a light that shines in a dark place, clearly pointing the way. It channels the path of the just toward the "day star" that arises in the hearts of believers (2 Peter 1:19). The Word of God dispels the darkness, the confusion, the ignorance, the fear, the superstition, and the dangers of the human situation.

The menorah symbolizes the very salvation of God, for we are told by the prophet that God would not rest until the salvation of his people be manifest as a lamp that burns brightly (Isaiah 62:1). Since God was referring to salvation and to his own lamp, could it have been anything other than the menorah? Understanding the menorah and the One whom it represents is a vision of God's salvation. Indeed, it is wisdom and knowledge in God's Word that brings stability and strengthens salvation (Isaiah 33:6). Without the stabilizing element of God's Word, the believer is left vulnerable to Satan's deceptive devices and to the ever-changing winds of teaching (Ephesians 4:14). With the Word of God's vision, the believer is grounded on a secure and stable foundation. Jesus declared that when one hears and does the Word of God ("these sayings of mine"), he wisely constructs his life on the bedrock of divine revelation and insight that will stand against every tumultuous circumstance life may bring (Luke 6:48).

It is the Word of God that causes the path of the just to be illuminated more and more until the day of completeness (Proverbs 4:18). The Word is the menorah that continues to dispel the darkness along the believer's pathway until it brings him to the light of noonday. When one sees the menorah, whether he be Jew or Christian, he should immediately recognize the fact that God has ordained a lamp for his anointed ones, his chosen people, to direct their paths and keep them safely in his way (Psalm 132:17). If God commissioned his Word as a menorah to lighten David's pathway, he will certainly do likewise for all believers.

The menorah is God's lamp and man's light because it is unique to God's character to give illumination, and it is essential to man's being that he have light. God is light, and in him is no darkness at all (1 John 1:5). If believers walk in the light as God is in the light, they have fellowship with one another and their sins are forgiven (1 John 1:7).

LET LIGHT BE!

The very first act in the creation of the present universe came with God's spoken Word: "Let light be." Suddenly in the universal darkness, light sprang forth, overwhelming the void of the universe with the pristine brightness of the Eternal. The sages have observed that when God saw "the light," he identified it with the Hebrew phrase *et ha-or*. When the numerical equivalents of the Hebrew letters for this phrase are totaled, the sum is 613, the exact number of commandments in the Torah (the Pentateuch). The sages have suggested that the light that pervaded the universe for three of creation's days before the formation of the sun, moon, and stars was the light of God's Word, the Torah. With this fundamental Hebraic understanding, the Apostle John's observations concerning the person and work of Jesus take on new significance: "In the beginning was the Word, and the Word was with God, and the Word was God. . . . In him was life, and the life was the light of men" (John 1:1, 4). If Jesus was the person of the Word of God as John declares, it is simple to understand him as the Torah incarnate, the primordial light that was manifest when God first spoke his Word.

Many Bible-believing people conceive of the universe as a closed system that God set into motion in eternity past when he completed his six days of creation. The beginning of that creation was the spoken Word: "Let light be." The truth is, however, that God did not just make this proclamation millennia ago. He speaks this creative word continually. His Word is the means by which the universe is sustained as Hebrews 1:3 declares: "[Jesus] being the brightness of his glory, and the express image of his person, and *upholding all things by the word of his power* . . ." He who eons ago said, "Let light be," is still making the same declaration so that all that exists is both created and sustained by the Word of God.

The fact that the Word of God and light are synonymous is confirmed in that both sound and light are of essentially the same energy. It is no mistake that many physicists now believe that all of matter was created from sound waves. Apparently the sound of God's Word that created light, the stuff of the universe, was the basis of energy and matter's substance. The instant that God sepa-

rated from himself the essence that he called the Word
(*Logos*), the creative process was set into motion in a dynamic that continues to the present time and will continue
forever. The light of God is manifest from the life that is
in the spoken and living Word.

The menorah is distinctive in that it represents this
light, the essence of the Divine nature. One of the most
frequently used metaphors that describe God in Scripture
is light. John simply declares, "God is light" (1 John 1:5).
Paul informs us that the Heavenly Father dwells in light
to which no man can approach, a light that envelops him
so that he is eternally unknown and unrevealed (1 Timothy 6:16). John tells us, moreover, that it is uniquely the
function of the Son of God, who became incarnate as Jesus
of Nazareth, to reveal the Father (John 1:18). This person
who was made flesh and tabernacled among men was the
Word of God, the life of whom was the light of men (John
1:4). In truth, Jesus was "the light of the world" (John
8:12).

A MESSIANIC PORTRAIT

In essence, the menorah can be seen as a perfect portrait of Jesus as Lord and Messiah. The *Logos* has historically been understood as an eternal light surrounding the
throne of God. Is it any wonder, then, that when John
viewed Jesus in his resurrected glory, he saw him in the
midst of seven golden lampstands, which may have been
either seven menorahs or one menorah of seven lamps
(Revelation 1:12-13)? The Messiah was indeed the light
enlightening every man. Paul succinctly encapsulates this
truth in 2 Corinthians 4:6: "For God, who commanded
the light to shine out of darkness, hath shined in our hearts,
to give the light of the knowledge of the glory of God in
the face of Jesus Christ." God in his transcendent essence
could not have been known except through revelation, as

the Epistle of Hebrews 1:1-3 teaches us: "God, who at sundry times and in divers manners spake in time past unto the fathers by the prophets, hath in these last days spoken unto us by his Son, whom he hath appointed heir of all things, by whom also he made the worlds; who being the brightness of his glory, and the express image of his person, and upholding all things by the word of his power, when he had by himself purged our sins, sat down on the right hand of the Majesty on high . . ."

According to Daniel 10:6, the Messiah would be one whose eyes would be as "lamps of fire." John saw this Messiah as Jesus in the midst of seven golden candlesticks (Revelation 1:12-13) and later as the Lamb with "seven horns and seven eyes" (Revelation 5:6). Zechariah also envisioned this same Messianic character who would be manifest as both priest and king (Zechariah 6:13), the Person who was a stone with "seven eyes" (Zechariah 4:9-10). The seven lamps of fire manifest in the menorah, then, are emblematic of the eyes of the Messiah, the Stone that the builders rejected who became the head of the corner (Matthew 21:42).

The menorah, then, is a perfect portrait of the Messiah, both in the Hebrew Scriptures and in the Apostolic Writings. He is uniquely the Living Menorah, the one who brings the pure, pristine light of the Eternal Presence into the hearts of those men who believe upon him.

WHY SEVEN?

The most obvious numerical quality of the menorah is seen in the seven lamps of fire atop the seven branches of the lampstand. The question that begs to be asked is, "Why seven?"

Seven in Holy Scripture is the number of both vision and power. This is seen in the Lamb of God in Revelation 5:6, who is described by John as having "seven horns and seven eyes," which are the "seven spirits of God." Horns are emblematic of power and authority while eyes are simply channels through which light is brought into the body. Zechariah describes these seven lamps of fire on the menorah as the "eyes of the Lord which run to and fro throughout the whole earth" (Zechariah 4:10). The number *seven*, then, manifests both power and illumination for vision.

As a power motif, seven is seen in the seven *shofarot* (ram's horns) that preceded the armies of Israel in their week-long daily circuit around the walls of Jericho. It is also seen in the secret of Samson's phenomenal physical prowess, the *seven* locks of hair on his head. It is no coincidence that there are seven angels with seven *shofarot*, seven thunders, and seven bowls of wrath in the apocalyptic vision of John (Revelation 8:2; 10:3; 15:7). These seven angels are equipped and authorized to manifest the power of God in judgment upon the earth in the time immediately preceding the Messianic Age.

Both the Apocalypse and the book of Isaiah tell us that there are seven spirits of God. Isaiah 11:2 lists them: the spirit of the Lord, the spirit of wisdom, the spirit of understanding, the spirit of counsel, the spirit of might, the spirit of knowledge, and the spirit of the fear of the Lord. In the Apocalypse, John served as an amanuensis for these seven spirits in conveying their personal messages to the seven churches in Asia Minor (Turkey). The concerns of these spirits in each of the churches help reveal their nature and function.

In reality, there is only one Spirit of God, just as there is only one Lord, one faith, and one baptism; however, that one Spirit of God operates in relationship to the universe and especially to mankind through seven channels. It is these seven channels that bring vision and insight to the people of God. It is also these operations that manifest the power of God for the preternatural in the lives of believers.

The Jewish people have always seen in the menorah the number of perfection or completeness. The six branches extending from the shaft of the menorah are emblematic of the six days of creation, while the central shaft and its perpetual light symbolize the Sabbath. Everything stems from the Creator; therefore, say the Jews, value is imparted to men's days from God's day of refreshment, *Shabbat* (the Sabbath). Holiness and perfection are achieved, not from men's days of work, but from the spiritual light emanating from God.

In a similar manner, the church has no righteousness, no splendor, no illumination except that which it receives from its attachment to the "Stem of Jesse," the Messiah. The church is the light of the world only to the extent that it is attached to Jesus and is imbued with his life and anointing. The fruit of life and light is found in the branches only as they are connected with the vine (John 15:1-5).

In Hebrew, the center lamp of the menorah is also called *ner Elohim* (the lamp of God) as well as *shamash* (helper). Both the central shaft and the center lamp are symbolic of God himself. Since the Scriptures teach that God is love, the center lamp may well represent the spirit of love. Love is the bond of completeness (Colossians 3:14); therefore, it is the element that maintains the perfection symbolized by the seven lamps.

ADDITIONAL SIGNIFICANT NUMBERS

An analysis of the menorah's structure also manifests other biblical numbers that are of significance to the believer. First, in the base of the menorah that was in the temple in 70 C.E., both the numbers *three* and *twelve* stand out. Rabbinic tradition and archaeology point to a tripod base. The number *three* represents the foundation of the Word of God, the *TaNaKh*–the *Torah* (Law), the *Nevi'im* (Prophets), and the *Ketuvim* (Writings)–the basis of Jesus' teachings in his ministry (Luke 24:44). The number *three* is also important to Christians who understand the very foundation of all light as God, who is manifest in three personalities.

The Arch of Titus depicts a menorah base made of two hexagonal platforms, making a total of twelve surfaces on which may have been inscribed the signs of the twelve tribes of Israel. The number *twelve* is significant in that it is the foundational number for much of God's activity among men. Twelve patriarchs were the foundation of the nation of Israel. Likewise, twelve apostles were the foundational pillars of the reformed congregation that is now called the church.

Secondly, in the various decorative elements of the menorah's branches the number *72* appears. There were three knops, three bowls, and three flowers (nine in all) in each of the six semicircular branches (a total of 54). The central shaft had four knops, bowls, and flowers (a total of 12). Added together, these produce 66, the exact number of books in the Christian canon of the Holy Scriptures. An additional knop was said to be under each of the extended branches of the menorah (a total of six). These, added to the 66, make a grand total of 72. (Some have suggested that these knops were included in the aforementioned on the central shaft. If this were the case, the six branches themselves added to the 66 ornaments would also total 72.) The number *72* is significant in that there were 70 elders who received the impartation of Moses' spirit by the laying on of hands and two who received the same spirit spontaneously in the camp (Numbers 11:16, 26). Interestingly enough, after Jesus had commissioned the twelve apostles, he also sent out 72 evangelists (prophets) before him (Luke 10:1).

In Israel's conquest of the Promised Land, seven priests led the way before the ark of the covenant, blowing *shofarot* announcing the fulfillment of God's promise to Moses. The same occurred in the New Testament church when seven men were chosen to administer the church's practical affairs. These were far more than "deacons" in the general sense of the word, for they included such powerful preachers of the Word as Stephen, whose profound apologetics resulted in the church's first martyr, and Philip, who was called "the evangelist" (Acts 21:8). Is it possible that they were chosen to represent the "seven spirits of God" in the body of Messiah? That the menorah with its seven lamps is a revelation of the church is clear from Proverbs 9:1: "Wisdom hath builded her house, she hath hewn out her seven pillars . . ." It is no coincidence that the spiritual house of God, the church, rested on twelve foundational pillars (the apostles–Ephesians 2:20) and seven pillars of wisdom (Acts 6:3).

The menorah, then, contains the pattern for leadership that was manifest in the New Testament church, upon which all of subsequent Christianity has been built. There were 12 foundational apostles, 72 prophets who proclaimed the good news, and seven men of wisdom. Through the teaching and practice of these men, the entire world has been illuminated by the light of truth. The church, then, has indeed been the "light of the world," the living menorah that has brought the understanding of Israel's God to the nations.

TRIMMED AND BURNING

The daily lighting of the lamps of the menorah was a carefully-orchestrated function of the temple priesthood. In the tabernacle in the wilderness, the lamps of the newly constructed menorah were cleaned by the priests in the morning and lit in the evening with the consecrated fire from the altar. Later tradition says that the center lamp of the menorah burned continuously, both day and night. It did not require additional oil, for it burned for 24 hours on the same amount of fuel that the other lamps required for 12 hours. This miracle was said to have continued unabated until the death of Simon the Just, the notable high priest and the last of the men of the Great Synagogue, exactly 40 years before the final destruction of the temple. Interestingly enough, tradition also says that the scarlet cord tied to the scapegoat failed to turn white on the Day of Atonement beginning exactly 40 years before the destruction of the temple. Both of these events were contemporaneous with the death, burial, and resurrection of Jesus.

Tradition from the days of the Second Temple suggests that the priests generally found two (according to the *Mishnah*) or even three (according to Josephus) of the menorah's lamps burning each morning, the two eastern lamps and the westernmost lamp. (The menorah stood on the south wall of the temple sanctuary opposite the table of shewbread; therefore, its lamps were arranged from east to west.) It is said that the lamp atop the central shaft of the menorah was turned in a westerly direction. From this "western lamp," the priests relit the other lamps at dusk. (If the western lamp was extinguished during the night, it was considered a bad omen.)

From the western lamp that burned continuously day and night, rabbinic Judaism has developed the *ner tamid*, the eternal flame (or perpetual light) which even now substitutes for the menorah in synagogues around the world. This everlasting light is a symbol of the ever-present God of whom it is said, "He that keepeth Israel shall neither slumber nor sleep" (Psalm 121:4). It also is a demonstration of uninterrupted worship on earth that parallels that which is practiced in heaven where the angelic hosts never cease exclaiming, "Holy, holy, holy, is the Lord God Almighty, who was, and is, and is to come" (Revelation 4:8; Isaiah 6:3).

It is also said that the menorah was positioned in such a way that it illuminated the table of shewbread that stood on the opposite wall of the sanctuary. This offered a vivid contrast between man's spiritual needs (light) and material needs (bread). It also demonstrated that the very Word of God (the bread of life) can be ingested and give sustenance to the human soul only when it is illuminated by the Eternal.

PURE GOLD, ONE BEATEN WORK

The menorah was to be one solid ingot of pure gold that was carved and hammered into the delicate candelabrum that has become such a magnificent living emblem. Each of these qualities and construction techniques is rich with symbolism to the believer, both Jew and Christian.

That it was to be of pure gold demonstrates the fact that God demands purity wherever light is manifest. Among the Jewish people, purity of motive is considered essential to worship. This is manifest in the intensity and concentration on the Divine called *kavanah*. Lackadaisical attitudes and ambivalence are never enlightening. Likewise, mere mindless repetition of words and actions leads only to darkness. When the Eternal is worshipped with a meek and contrite heart, prayer is efficacious.

In order to acquire "pure gold" one must subject the precious metal to the refiner's fire seven times. This underscores the fact that only those who will permit God to "turn up the heat" that causes the dross and impurities to rise to the surface where they can be removed will find themselves becoming the "pure gold" of which the living menorah must be constructed. This is that part of Israel and/or the church which the prophet predicted would be brought through the fire and refined (Zechariah 13:9). It is only by the trials of the Word of God and the testing that God allows to come to our lives (like Abraham's testing) that purity is manifest in our hearts.

This is why Jews do not approach God thinking to impress him with the splendor of their dress or external appearance (as the Gentile cultures have done in worshipping their deities). The adornment of a meek and quiet spirit is far more impressive in the presence of God (1 Peter 3:3-4). They wear a simple white prayer shawl, which they see as a "garment of light." Complete focus on the majesty and holiness of the Eternal is the aim of worship among the Jewish people. These are the *haredim*, those who tremble in the presence of God. The central idea in Judaism is to "revere," not "understand" God. The goal is to "know" God, not "know about God." Worship is not worship without *kavanah*.

This truth was emphasized by Jesus: ". . . true worshippers shall worship the Father in spirit and in truth" (John 4:23). It is manifest in the Hebrew and Greek words for worship, both of which mean to prostrate oneself in the presence of the King. It is the "pure in heart" who will "see God" (Matthew 5:8). Every man who has the hope of salvation "purifieth himself," even as God is pure (1 John 3:3). The wisdom that is from above is "first pure" (James 3:17). Those who seek God with *kavanah* find that they are processed by the Holy Spirit in the refiner's fire that brings them forth as pure gold. God told Zechariah of a people whom he would "refine . . . as silver is refined" and whom he would "try . . . as gold is tried," so that when the process is completed, God will say of them, "It is my people" (Zechariah 13:9).

In the ancient world, gold was the most precious of metals, prized by people of power and prestige. Accordingly, gold was used in ancient Israel to symbolize the high value placed by Israelite society on personal and communal worship of God Almighty. The golden candelabrum is symbolic of the priceless nature of the enlightenment that

God brings to those who fear him. We are commanded by Jesus to "buy the truth" and sell it not. There is always a price to be paid for truth, sometimes the ultimate price.

That the menorah was of one piece certainly stresses the idea of oneness, both in God and in the company of his people, Israel and the church. Paul stressed this truth: "There is one Lord, one faith, one baptism, one God and Father of all, who is above all, and in you all" (Ephesians 4:5-6). In Romans 12:5, the apostle explained this oneness in the church: "So we, being many, are one body in Christ, and every one members one of another." The oneness of God's congregation is a reflection of the oneness of the Eternal. The first and greatest commandment is the *Shema*: "Hear, O Israel, the Lord our God, is one Lord." It was only proper, then, that Jesus' final prayer was that his disciples would be "one" even as Jesus and the Father are one (John 17:21-22).

Just as the menorah featured many decorations and distinctive parts yet was made of one piece of gold, so the body of Christ is one, manifesting itself in a diversity of expressions. The unity of which the Holy Spirit is the agent (Ephesians 4:3) is the cohesiveness that binds the millions of atoms of pure gold together in the one ingot that, consequently, is fashioned as the light of the world, the pure, beaten, one-piece menorah.

Every microscopic particle of gold has the potential for being the light of the world. When believers are connected to the Word of God, to Jesus, who is God's light, and when they permit the Holy Spirit to purify them and fill them with the oil of his gladness, then they will be lights in a world of darkness.

THE TREE OF LIFE

The parallel in appearance between the menorah and a tree is not coincidental. The shape of the menorah with

its branches extending from a central shaft is clearly patterned after a tree. The Jewish people believe that the
menorah originally represented the tree of life. The connection between the lampstand and the Word of God as
David's "lamp unto my feet," and the Torah as a tree of
life is clear. Solomon declared that wisdom is a "tree of
life" (Proverbs 3:18). Even in the Apocalypse, God says
that they "who do his commandments" have a right "to
the tree of life" (Revelation 22:14).

The blending of tree and fire motifs is clearly seen in
the profound burning bush incident, initiating the process
that resulted in the establishment of the chosen people.
Moses was called and commissioned by God himself by
divine words spoken from a bush that was burning but
was not consumed. Perhaps this was a preliminary manifestation of the rich symbolism of the menorah to the
prophet who would liberate Israel. The fire of the *Shekhinah* was manifested in a bush, and from that fire came the
Word of God. The menorah likewise appears as a golden
tree from which fire is manifest to bring light and life
through God's Word.

It is no coincidence that the imagery employed in the
design of the candlestick is that of almonds, the first trees
to bloom and produce fruit in Israel in the spring. The flowers on the branches were almond flowers and the knops
were almonds. Perhaps this motif is connected with the
miraculous budding of Aaron's almond rod when the question of divine right to priesthood arose (Numbers 17:6).
In the dead, desiccated rod's bringing forth new life is seen
a symbol of the resurrection. The menorah as the tree of
life symbolically brings life through the light of its lamps.

The Hebrew word for "almond" is from the root
shakod, which also means "watching." This idea is set forth
in Jeremiah 1:11-12 where the prophet was given a vision
of an almond branch and was assured by the Eternal: "I

am watching to see that my words come true." The juxta-position of the words *almond* and *watching* is clear. Because the menorah is intrinsically tied with the almond tree, it is a symbol of God's vigilance to provide eternal light for his people as well as an indication of their prevailing before him with unceasing prayer (1 Thessalonians 5:17).

The almond rods of the twelve leaders of Israel were also used in one instance to dig a well of water (Numbers 21:18). This, again, is a symbol of the manifestation of the water of life through the agency of the almond tree. It is also noteworthy that true biblical authority (leadership) is always manifest in the bringing forth of life (the water of the Holy Spirit).

The menorah is a symbol of arborescent Israel, the nation which was God's family tree of salvation and cov-enant relationship. In Romans 11 Paul used the metaphor of the productive olive tree to describe ancient Israel. In Joel 1:7, Israel is likened to the fig tree. It is fitting, there-fore, that the menorah has historically been the most promi-nent symbol of the Jewish people as a nation. Though the Star of David has been popular in the past two centuries, the menorah has remained the material emblem *par excel-lence* for the Jewish people.

It is no coincidence also that the two wooden dowels on which Torah scrolls are wound are called *etz hayim* (tree of life). The Torah is the record of God's instructions that produce life when they are fulfilled. Walking in rebellion to the commandments of God encapsulated in the Torah tends toward death. Walking in faithfulness to the *halachah* that is established in the Torah is a life-giving exercise.

The menorah is also said to reflect the shape of the moriah plant in Israel, which naturally releases its fragrance in the heat of the day when the sun reaches its zenith and radiates the most intense light of the day. Light and fra-grance were brought together in the menorah and the burning of incense in the temple.

The menorah is also a symbol of the arborescent Messiah, the long-expected ruler in Israel who would come from the stem of Jesse (Isaiah 11:1) and be the Branch of the Lord (Zechariah 3:8). It has been suggested that the earliest believers in Jesus as Messiah were styled "*Notzrim*" because they were followers of the *Netzer*, the branch from the root of Jesse. It is quite appropriate that the glorified Jesus was seen by the Revelator in the midst of the menorah (seven golden lampstands). The Messiah is the Tree of Life, and the life that is inherent in his being is the light of men (John 1:4).

Even without its lamps of fire, then, the menorah *per se* is filled with rich significance, demonstrating the tree of life manifest in the Garden of Eden, but now revealed in the light of the world, the Word of God. It is of no small consequence that such an object, representing the tree of life that was first in Eden and finally appearing in heaven in the Bible's last chapter, was placed in Israel's tent of meeting and all subsequent sanctuaries. Only in the light of God's Word is there eternal life.

BOTH SYNAGOGUE AND CHURCH STILL ABLAZE

In spite of widespread apostasy in the world today, a large number of believers who are biblicists stand squarely and unequivocally for the divine truth that is represented in the Word of God. In some cases, Jews outshine Christians when it comes to upholding biblical morality and ethics. One only need cite the example of Jewish students who recently challenged the requirements of formerly "Christian" Yale University that forced them to live in dormitories where fornication and other sexual immorality were encouraged by the system and flaunted by their fellow students. There is also the case of the young Jewish girl who was so affronted by the lack of modesty at formerly "Christian" Princeton University that she created a media frenzy by insisting that modesty is preferable to outright lasciviousness.

On the other hand, there are millions of Christians in thousands of congregations around the world who have been labeled extremists by the secular media because they insist on believing and practicing the absolute ethics of the Ten Commandments rather than participating in the situational ethics of consequentialism promoted by an increasingly hostile, humanistic society and its governmental agencies. When evil abounds, grace is much more abundant (Romans 5:20). When darkness is at its thickest and most pervasive, light radiates forth as a beacon of hope to the lost and dying. Even the smallest flickering candle is enlightening in abject darkness. The age-old confrontation between the sons of light and the sons of darkness that so captivated the imagination of the Qumran community of first-century Israel is growing larger and larger.

Part of the strategy of the realm of darkness is an attempt to substitute darkness for light, bitter for sweet, and evil for good. Such was the lamentation of Isaiah 5:20: "Woe unto them that call evil good, and good evil; that put darkness for light, and light for darkness; that put bitter for sweet, and sweet for bitter!" What is patently evil is championed as good, for liberated modern men and women must be free to do anything that their hearts imagine. But an even greater evil follows the same path as in Isaiah's day: "[They] justify the wicked for reward, and take away the righteousness of the righteous from him!" (Isaiah 5:23). The right conduct spelled out in the Word of God is so disparaged that many begin to question it and eventually have it taken away from them by the challenges of evil and by their own fears of being ostracized as nonconformists.

Throughout history, however, millions of Jews and Christians have faced such challenges, refusing to compromise with the darkness that causes light to be extinguished. Their fiery passion for the Eternal cannot be quenched by even the most pervasive darkness and wickedness. They become living firebrands of the good news that God's kingdom will ultimately triumph over all evil. These are the living menorahs, the living emblems of truth and righteousness who shine as lights in a wicked and perverse generation (Philippians 2:15).

BY MY SPIRIT, SAITH THE LORD

When the men of Judah were confronted with the arduous task of rebuilding Jerusalem and the temple, they were given a divine word of encouragement and consolation by Zechariah the prophet: "Not by might, nor by power, but by my spirit, saith the Lord of hosts" (Zechariah 4:6). Accompanying this prophetic pronouncement was a magnificent vision, a panorama of symbols that the political and spiritual leaders of Judah readily understood. The prophet was shown a menorah that was burning brightly, abundantly supplied with oil from two olive trees adjacent to it. Though a great mountain of opposition stood before Zerubbabel, the governor, and Joshua, the high priest, God's promise was that it would become a plain. Perhaps the imagery was the same as Daniel's prediction that the kingdom of God would be established when a stone hewn out of the mountain would crush the image of idolatry (Daniel 2:45).

The message is as clear now as it was then: it is not by military prowess or by the power of men that ultimate victory is achieved. It is only a result of the Holy Spirit's manifestation in the midst of his people. It is the menorah's light that crushes darkness, reducing the mountain of doubt and of human and demonic opposition to the dust of a plain. God will always have anointed vessels through whom he will provide the pure beaten olive oil that makes the menorah burn brightly. It is by God's Spirit, not man's strength.

This metaphor could not be more significant than at the present time, when preparation for the Messianic Age signals a time of restoration (Acts 3:20-21) very much parallel to that which was occurring in Zechariah's day. Like Ezra, Nehemiah, Zerubbabel, Joshua, Haggai, and Zechariah, today's restorers are demanding the rebuilding of the ancient City of God, which a great King in Israel, Yeshua HaMashiach, established centuries ago (Ezra 5:11). Their identity is simple: "We are the servants of the God of heaven and earth." No egomaniacal jockeying for power, prestige, or perquisites here, no private agendas or personal kingdom-building, no dwelling in "paneled houses" while God's house lies waste (Haggai 1:4)! The identity of these people is in bond-slavery to God, and their mission is simple: restoring the biblical congregation to be the City of God.

This restoration is encapsulated in the paradigm of the menorah–God's lamp, man's light. It is a work that even now is expanding exponentially as the Holy Spirit (". . . by my spirit, saith the Lord") summons the church to restore the ancient paths wherein are the good ways of God. The menorah is a living emblem that demonstrates to the church and synagogue that the pure olive oil of the Holy Spirit will bring forth the light of eternity to guide people on this planet until the time of the Messiah.

Restoration and rededication always produce light. This was the case when the Maccabees rededicated and restored the menorah following the idolatry of Antiochus Epiphanes and his planned Hellenization of Israel. When the menorah was rededicated, the remaining one-day's supply of consecrated oil burned miraculously for eight days (the time required for new oil to be produced and consecrated). Is this not a paradigm for the church today? The oil that remains will burn miraculously when the church is dedicated to restoration. A simple axiom of history is this: "Dedication produces light."

DISPLAY IN HOME AND SANCTUARY

While there is a long-standing tradition in Judaism that does not permit the use of the menorah in public worship, there is no biblical prohibition regarding its use as a symbol and implement of faith. Rabbinic Judaism has substituted the "eternal flame" for the menorah in synagogues, and many Christian communions have followed this tradition in their sanctuaries (though most are likely unaware of its origin).

Many churches use candelabra of various sorts during ceremonies and worship, and these are certainly legitimate visual displays. The menorah, however, is a living emblem of profound and continuing significance to Christians. While the ancient menorah has been lost in antiquity, the emblem remains viable. The fact that Solomon constructed ten *menorot* and placed five on both sides of the entrance leading to the Holy of Holies is evidence that copies or models may be legitimately employed in worship services.

A parade of history's tyrants has sought to destroy the menorah. First, Nebuchadnezzar may have taken the temple menorah along with other vessels when he looted Solomon's temple. Then, Antiochus Epiphanes destroyed the menorah in his attempt to replace the light of monotheism in Jerusalem with Hellenism. The Maccabean menorah was likely made of some inferior material; however, the religious significance of that menorah was perhaps even greater than its predecessors, considering the miracle of light that occurred at its dedication (*hanukkah*).

Later, in Herod's grandiose attempt to supersede the splendor of Solomon's temple, he constructed a new and glorious menorah, said to be six feet in height and three feet in width, with branches four inches thick. This menorah was probably part of the spoils of war that Titus deposited in Rome's Temple of Peace. When the vandals subsequently plundered Rome, they carried the menorah to Carthage only to have it removed to Byzantium by Justinian. A Jew there convinced Justinian that the menorah should be returned to Palestine where it was kept in the custody of the Christian community. When the Persians later captured Jerusalem in the seventh century, they plundered the Christian sanctuaries. Since that time, there is no information as to the menorah's whereabouts. Legends suggest that it was secreted away by holy men, much as tradition purports that the original temple menorah was hidden, perhaps by Jeremiah, before Nebuchadnezzar's invasion.

It may well be that both temporal and spiritual "powers and principalities" have sought to deny believers the use of history's greatest living emblem. It is the piety of the Jewish sages who insisted that nothing originally standing in the temple may be reproduced until it is needed for the Third Temple that has militated against the more frequent and open use of this living emblem. That it was a strong symbol in synagogues of Jesus' time is clear from his own reference to the light of the world on a candlestick (Matthew 5:14) and from the Apocalypse's imagery, both in the view of the glorified Messiah and in the positioning of the "lampstand" in the Ephesian church (Revelation 2:5).

Since each home is to be a *mikdash me'at* (mini-sanctuary), it would seem quite appropriate that believers should have a menorah in their homes to symbolize the divine light of the sanctuary. This living emblem would offer great spiritual insight and object lessons for devotion and study. The menorah should be more than a mantelpiece decoration, however. It should be an honored symbol, a material demonstration of Jesus the Messiah as the light of the world.

If the menorah was used in the Gentile church at Ephesus, it is certainly appropriate for use in the sanctuaries of all communions today. This is an excellent way to demonstrate the continuity of the church with the ancient congregation of God among the Jews. It is a means of clearly manifesting the roots of Christian faith in biblical and Second Temple Judaism. If the lighting of the lamps in the tent of meeting and in all subsequent sanctuaries of Judaism was appropriate in demonstrating the Divine Presence among God's chosen people, then it certainly should remain so today. After all, "Jesus Christ [is] the same, yesterday, and today, and for ever" (Hebrews 13:8).

Chapter 4

The Mezuzah

One of the most ubiquitous and readily observable mnemonic devices in Judaism is the *mezuzah*, the rectangular box that is attached to the right doorpost of the entrance to every observant Jewish home and to every habitable room of therein. Available in myriads of sizes and styles that reflect the taste of the owner, each *mezuzah* is a signpost on the door of the Jewish home that proclaims it a household separated unto God and his service.

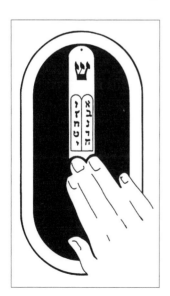

This sacred symbol reminds the Jew of his obligation to abide by the Word of God's commandments and to transmit its understanding to succeeding generations. It also demonstrates God's ever present protection of his people. By it, Jews affirm their belief in the truth of prophecy, the creation of the world, and divine providence.

THE BIBLICAL BASIS

All *mezuzot* have one thing in common: they function as a container for a piece of parchment on which is inscribed the text of the Hebrew Scriptures that declares: "Hear, O Israel: The Lord our God is one Lord: and thou shalt love the Lord thy God with all thine heart, and with all thy soul, and with all thy might. And these words, which I command thee this day, shall be in thine heart: And thou shalt teach them diligently unto thy children, and shalt talk of them when thou sittest in thine house, and when thou walkest by the way, and when thou liest down, and when thou risest up. And thou shalt bind them for a sign upon thine hand, and they shall be as frontlets between thine eyes. And thou shalt write them upon the posts of thy house, and on thy gates" (Deuteronomy 6:4-9). "And thou shalt write them upon the door posts of thine house, and upon thy gates" (Deuteronomy 11:20).

The greatest of all God's commandments to Israel is the *Shema* ("Hear, O Israel: the Lord our God is one Lord"), the statement that forever establishes monotheism, the understanding that there is but *one* God. Jesus affirmed the primacy of the *Shema* (Mark 12:29-30). Monotheism, an uncommon and unique understanding in the ancient world, came to the Israelites as a result of God's revelation to Abraham more than four centuries before the Sinai event. Abraham was a Gentile, a Babylonian by birth and a Syrian by nationality. While Abraham was in this thoroughly pagan Gentile environment, constructing idols for those who worshipped the pantheon of deities featured in the polytheistic system of Babylon, he discovered by revelation that those gods were no gods at all and that there was only *one* God, the Eternal Creator who, unlike the material representations of the pagan gods, was invisible. After the death of Abraham's father, he received the simple commandment of God: "*Lech lekha!*" ("Go unto yourself!"–i.e. into your own inner spiritual resources). Abraham responded in faith, crossing over the River Euphrates and entering the Promised Land. With this act of faith, he became the first Hebrew (from *eber*, to cross over) and the father of the faithful–indeed, of us all (Romans 4:16). Abraham was the first to "cross over" the waters, i.e. to realize the essential godliness and spirituality of human existence.

One of the reasons God established a covenantal relationship with Abraham is stated in Genesis 18:19: "I know him [Abraham], that he will command his children and his household after him, and they shall keep the way of the Lord, to do justice and judgment." It was, therefore, a part of Abraham's life style, as well as that of his descendants, to perpetuate the knowledge of the ways of God in every generation. Whatever devices proved to be an aid in accomplishing this effort were employed.

A BADGE OF HONOR

It was only proper, then, that when the time came for God to establish forever the unique statement concerning his very essence, "the Lord is One," as the overarching principle of his instruction to his people, he would enjoin the use of various devices that would instantly call to remembrance to every observant descendant of Abraham the fundamental truth that God had revealed. Hence, the use of the *mezuzah*, to write on every doorpost and gate (with a lintel) in the community of Israel the words of this commandment, a badge of honor at the entrance of every Jewish household proclaiming the sovereignty of God Almighty. The Jewish response was the construction of a device to house the words of the commandment in a clearly visible form, a silent sentry, as it were, that would constantly remind each Jew who passed through the door of the house or gate that led to the Jewish house that God is *one* and that his commandments are to be remembered and fulfilled.

Through the centuries, the *mezuzah* has been a con-

stant reminder to the Jewish people of their responsibility
to proclaim the absolute ethics that God has entrusted to
them as a people. Whenever a Jew passes through the door
of a Jewish home, he is reminded of his own Jewishness
and of the great Jewish ideals that his Jewishness espouses.
The *mezuzah* silently declares, "You are under the authority of the Torah, and wherever you may be, your life must
demonstrate God's righteousness and holiness, the integrity of his morality." Observant Jews, both upon either
entering or leaving their homes, touch the *mezuzah*, and
kiss their fingertips. In some Jewish *minhagim* (regional traditions), an observant Jew may also recite the verse, "May
God keep my going out and my coming in from now on
and for ever more," a passage taken from the text of Psalm
121:8.

Throughout history, the Jewish people have diligently
fulfilled the commandment of the *mezuzah* and have viewed
it as a badge of honor. They have faithfully attached *mezuzot*
to their doorposts even when doing so readily identified
them as Jews and practitioners of Judaism to their mortal
enemies. This was especially true in Europe during the
time of the Third Reich when many pious Jews refused to
hide their identity by removing the *mezuzot* from their doorposts.

SENTRY AT THE THRESHOLD

In the ancient world, much superstition was connected
with entering through the door of a house. In many societies, it was considered an evil omen to come into contact
with the threshold of the door. Marco Polo reported that
in China guards were stationed at the doors of important
facilities to ensure the fact that no one stepped on the
threshold. Considerable punishment was inflicted upon
those who violated the protocol. This is where the custom
of jumping over the threshold originated and is likely the

basis for the practice of carrying one's bride over the threshold.

While this tradition may not have impacted the Israelites directly, they did place importance upon the entrance of their houses. Indeed, the temple in Jerusalem had a special officer: the "keeper of the threshold." Israel's "goings in" and "comings out" were to be blessed and preserved. Many important actions occurred at the gates of a city and at the door to a house. In the city gates, the elders assembled to transact city business and adjudicate legal matters. At the door of a house a slave who had been released who wished to remain as a "voluntary slave" had his ear pierced and a ring inserted. Perhaps in answer to the superstitions of the surrounding cultures, God commanded the Israelites to write this law of freedom on the entrances to their houses.

Though a silent sentry, the *mezuzah* has always been a very vocal preacher. Like Jeremiah of old, crying aloud and sparing not, lifting up the voice like a trumpet, it has summoned those who pass over the threshold of a Jewish home or public gathering place to remember their responsibility to God and to his Word in fulfilling the commandments of the Torah. The *mezuzah*'s 22 lines (corresponding to the 22 letters of the Hebrew alphabet) are chosen from the Torah's 4,875 verses to form a powerful encapsulation of Judaism. Because it graces the entry to the Jewish home, it establishes God's Torah in each home, guaranteeing the survival of the Jewish home and of the community of Israel.

Interestingly enough, though one is not expected to open the box and read the scroll, its message is thunderously clear. Each person who views the *mezuzah* is reminded that God is *one* and that every believer is to worship God with all his heart, soul, and might. He is repeatedly told that he is to remember and do all the commandments and be holy unto God. The time frame for this exercise is "when thou sittest in thy house, when thou walkest by the way, when thou liest down and when thou risest up" (Deuteronomy 6:7). He is also specifically reminded of God's command that he teach these precepts diligently to his children.

A *mezuzah* on the doorpost, then, has a profound power. It signals that what was a mere house has become a Jewish home and, in effect, a *mikdash me'at*, a mini-temple, where men and God dwell together in communion. Its very presence in clearly visible form on the doors of the home guides the Jewish family toward the heritage of a life of reverence to God.

THE DOORPOST MARKER

The Hebrew word *mezuzah*, which literally means "doorpost," is the word that appears in the Torah text: ". . . write [this command–the *Shema*] on the *mezuzah* [doorpost] of your house and upon your gates." The etymological root of *mezuzah* is the Hebrew *zv*, which means "tall, erect, or prominent." The Jewish people have chosen to name their material application of God's commandment with the word describing the location where they are to write the commandment: *mezuzah*.

The *mezuzah* is comprised of two parts: the container and the parchment. The container may be of practically any material: wood, brass, silver, ceramic, glass, or any other that may be formed into a box. Generally, the container is inscribed in some manner with the Hebrew letter *shin*, which has come to be a symbol for the Divine. One of God's names is *El Shaddai*, which means, "The Almighty." Rashi has noted that the Hebrew word *dai* means "enough" (as in the Passover *seder* hymn *Dayyenu*: "It [would have] sufficed us"). The Mishnaic Hebrew relative pronoun *she-*, "that, who, which," prefixed to *dai* renders, "who is enough," i.e. "who alone is sufficient." *'El She-ddai*, then,

means, "God, who is sufficient." Everything else ultimately
depends on him. He alone is self-sufficing, and He alone is
enough for all of creation's needs.

The significance of the *shin* in the *mezuzah* as a symbol for God is seen in the literal, material fulfillment of
God's statement regarding the placement of his name. In
1 Kings 11:36, God declared that Jerusalem is "the city
which I have chosen me to put my name there." It is striking that the three valleys that circumscribe and intersect
the city of Jerusalem (the Kidron, the Hinnom, and the
Tyropoeon) form the Hebrew letter *shin*. Any topographi-
cal map or aerial photograph of Jerusalem will confirm
this fact. God, therefore, placed his name (represented by
the letter *shin*) on Jerusalem in the very topography of the
city. When Jewish families place *mezuzot* on the doorposts
of their homes, they are, in effect, placing the name of
God, *El Shaddai*, at every entry to their dwelling.

In many cases, the container of the *mezuzah* is inscribed with the entire name *Shaddai*, using the letters *shin*,
daleth, *yod*. Interestingly enough, these letters also form an
acronym for *shomer daltot Yisrael*, which means "guardian
of the doors of Israel," a statement that it is *El Shaddai*
who is the guardian of the homes of the Jewish people.

The second and most important part of the *mezuzah*
is called the *klaf* (parch-
ment), a dried skin on
which a *sofer* (scribe) has
inscribed by hand in He-
brew the words of the
commandment in Deuter-
onomy 6:4-9 and 11:12-
21. Originally, these
passages were likely written directly on the door-
posts of Israelite homes;

–Ancient Mezuzah Klaf

however, as the practice was formalized, a thoroughgoing tradition for inscribing the biblical words and attaching them to the doorposts emerged. This custom traces to biblical times, for the use of a *mezuzah* case is mentioned in the Talmud (*Baba Metzia*, 102a).

The Hebrew words on the *klaf* are transcribed in a specific manner, line for line, on twenty-two lines. If a single mistake is made, the entire parchment is *pasul* (invalid) and may not be used. Unlike the Torah scroll itself, the *klaf* of the *mezuzah* may be inscribed from memory by the *sofer*. When a *mezuzah* is constructed in the above manner, with the appropriate inscription, it is termed *kosher* and is acceptable according to the *halakhah* (manner of walking or acceptable behavior) of scriptural and rabbinic tradition. The *halakhah* does not permit printed versions of the inscriptions, for the Torah specifies that you shall *write* the commandment on your doorpost. On the back of the parchment is written the name *Shaddai* (Almighty), which may be made visible by a small opening in the container. The custom of inscribing *Shaddai* on the *klaf* originated in the *Zohar*, became standard practice in the Middle Ages, and continues to the present day. This commandment is more often fulfilled by having the Hebrew letter *shin* displayed on the box itself.

MEZUZAH MISUNDERSTANDINGS

Many Christian theologians, pastors, and Bible teachers have considered the literalist interpretation of God's commandment to be legalistic, an effort to gain acceptance before God by works. The *mezuzah*, they have thought, is nothing more than an attempt to be accepted by God on the basis of externals (what is done) rather than on the basis of internals (what is believed). The truth is that affixing *mezuzot* on the doorposts of one's dwelling is far more biblical than many of the outward symbols which the church uses to reveal and manifest spiritual things about Jesus and Christian faith. While every visible manifestation that reveals an invisible truth is acceptable, those material objects that are either commanded by God or designed by man in response to God's instructions, whether literal or figurative, are particularly apropos.

Others have suggested that the *mezuzah* is merely a good luck charm, talisman, or amulet, as it were, designed to ward off evil spirits. Perhaps in some Jewish homes, particularly in medieval times when the general populace, including most Christians, was indeed superstitious, some Jewish people may have looked upon the *mezuzah* in this manner. The greatest of Judaism's teachers, however, have emphatically stated that to think of the *mezuzah* as an amulet is to distort and pervert its meaning and function. The vast majority of observant Jewish homes, therefore, affix *mezuzot* to their doorposts as a means of fulfilling the *mitzvah* that God gave to their patriarchs and matriarchs centuries ago and of providing a constant reminder to their families of the importance of remembering the commandments of God's Word.

JESUS, THE LIVING MEZUZAH

Jesus was a living *Mezuzah*, the embodiment of the Word of God who pointed and marked the way to eternal life. He was an incarnational manifestation of *El Shaddai*, the Almighty. He was the Word of God made flesh, the living Torah deposited in a container of clay. His face bore the likeness of the invisible God, for he was the express image of God's person and the brightness of his glory (Hebrews 1:1-2). The glory of God's name was seen in the face of Jesus Christ (2 Corinthians 4:6). He confessed that "he that has seen me has seen the Father" (John 14:9). His body was a container for the Word of God, a visible manifestation that put a face on the Father. Jesus is not only the doorpost; he is the very door itself, the portal to eternal life (John 10:7).

In reality, God wants every believer to become a living *mezuzah*, a container that is stamped with his name and filled with his Word. Indeed, those who are victorious are said to have the Father's name inscribed in their foreheads, at the top and on the front of the physical containers of their souls (Revelation 3:12; 14:1). Every true believer will be as David, having hidden the Word of God in his heart that he might not sin against the Almighty (Psalm 119:11; Romans 10:8). He will seek to be a living epistle of God, known and read of all men (2 Corinthians 3:2). If one is, indeed, living the lifestyle of obedience to God's Word, he becomes a manifestation of the Word of God, a light in the world, holding forth the word of life (Philippians 2:15-16). In effect, he becomes a living *mezuzah*, like Jesus, marking and pointing out the narrow gate to eternal life and relationship with God for all who pass by (Matthew 7:14).

Recognizing in the *mezuzah* a symbol of Jesus in no way diminishes or replaces the importance of the *mezuzah* for the Jewish people or for Christians. By affixing this instrument to their doorposts, Jews are fulfilling a simple commandment of God himself. By so doing, they signal their honor of both God and his Word. Jesus did not supersede the requirements of the Torah. As a matter of fact, he participated fully in this fulfillment of God's commandments. Christian recognition of Jesus in the symbolism of the *mezuzah* merely enhances their respect for the symbol's rich meaning for the Jewish people.

Jesus was the Word of God incarnate, the fullest disclosure of the person and nature of God himself. As a result of his offering himself as a sacrifice for sin for the entire human race, men who have faith in God's provision through him are fully reconciled unto God, justified by grace through faith in God's once-and-for-all provision for salvation. Those who have believed upon him have also received the indwelling of the Holy Spirit, the Lawgiver himself, who has written God's laws upon their hearts and imparted unto them the power to walk in the Spirit, thereby establishing and fulfilling the law of God.

CHRISTIAN PARTICIPATION

Can Christians share in this biblically Judaic practice? Some would suggest that if Christians were to do so, they would be expropriating a Jewish practice for their own reasons; however, in reality, any Christian who would choose to affix *mezuzot* to the doorposts or gates of his home would simply be imitating the lifestyle of Jesus and the apostles, all of whom would have fulfilled this ancient Jewish practice, which dates at least to the time of Ezra and the beginning of Second Temple Judaism.

Is there any reason why a Christian would not want to imitate the life of Jesus and do the things that he did? While there is certainly no requirement that a Christian engage in this practice, there is nothing that would restrict him from doing so. It is certainly not a means of achieving or even maintaining status before God (righteousness); however, it can be a significant reminder to one's family of the importance of believing and fulfilling the Word of God both individually and corporately as a family. It is no different from having a cross or a picture of Jesus in one's home or having various visible symbols in a sanctuary for corporate worship.

The *mezuzah* is merely another part of the rich heritage to which a Christian becomes entitled when he comes to faith in Jesus. If one is attached to the Jewish roots of the Christian faith and is a fellow citizen with the chosen of Israel, then he is entitled to the heritage of that citizenship and relationship.

Christians who choose to employ this part of the ancient Judaic heritage to which they have become entitled by virtue of their faith in Jesus should do so as a reminder of their faith in God to be a doer of his word, not just a hearer only. Each time they see the *mezuzah* on their doorposts, they should recall that the living Word of God lives in their hearts by the Holy Spirit, empowering them to fulfill the teachings of the written Word, a portion of which is integral to the *mezuzah*.

In what better way can a Christian signal to himself, to his family, and to everyone who visits his home that he is committed to the fulfillment of God's Word in his life, in his family, and in his community of faith (the church) than by affixing a visible symbol on his doorpost–a *mezuzah*? Of course, one should be careful to display a *mezuzah* with respect to his Jewish neighbors by doing so properly and honorably. In doing so, one can also demonstrate his solidarity with the international Jewish community in the spirit of Ruth, the Gentile woman who proclaimed to Naomi, her Jewish mother-in-law: "Your people shall be my people, your God shall be my God . . . and where you die, I will die" (Ruth 1:16-17).

A *mezuzah* may be attached to the doorpost at the entry to a house or on a gate (on the right as one enters the door, according to *Yoma* 11b). It may also be attached to any interior doorpost in a house (except bathrooms, closets, cabinets, and the like). Measuring from the lintel of the door, it is placed at a point approximating one-third of the distance from the top of the door to the bottom (*Menachot* 33a). If a door is unusually high, it is affixed at the level of a man's shoulder. It is always in a vertical position, inclined inward (rather than standing erect) as a sign that even the Word of God bows in the presence of the Eternal (Rashi, *Avida kesikta*, *Menachot* 33a). A small ceremony called *Hanukkat Ha-Bayit* (dedication of the house) accompanies the affixing of the *mezuzah*. Prior to attaching a *mezuzah* to the doorpost, one repeats the benediction: "Blessed are you, O Lord our God, King of the universe, who has commanded us to affix a *mezuzah*."

A LIVING EMBLEM

In reality, each observant Jew who employs the *mezuzah* is showing his respect for the commandments of God that outline the Word of God in practical demonstrations. Knowing the forgetfulness of humankind, God has provided instruments for remembrance, including the *mezuzah*. The various remembrance devices that God gave to Israel are part of his profound wisdom that enables his people to be in the world but not of the world, to transcend human tendencies and to be elevated into a face-to-face relationship with the Divine. In order to walk in this spiritual realm, we must be continually reminded to overcome life's distractions and to focus our attention on God. The Torah lifestyle, therefore, features predesigned and built-in reminders of God's Word and his promises to mankind. For traditional Jews, these mnemonic symbols continually reestablish their identity as God's chosen people, confirming the fact that God never ceases to watch over their homes, implanting the belief in the Almighty, the guardian of Israel, in their hearts, and providing visible evidence that they maintain belief in the Unity of God.

For Christians, these devices are reminders that they have become new creations through faith in Israel's Messiah and as such are members of God's family, the community of faith. For both Jew and Christian a *mezuzah* is a living emblem, pointing to a greater and deeper reality, the submission of the home as society's fundamental unit to the direction and protection of the Eternal God. It is another of the thoughtful benefits that God has provided for his people to remind them of their relationship with him and of their responsibility to reflect his attributes through their lives into the lives of others. A small box with a concealed parchment, the *mezuzah* is no insignificant device. Indeed, it is a concise proclamation of the message of dynamic faith manifest in the Judaism in which Jesus and the apostles lived their lives and expressed their devotion to God.

Chapter 5

The Tallit

When one thinks of Jews and worship, the image that immediately comes to mind is that of the Jewish man wrapped in his *tallit* (prayer shawl) and engaged in prayer to the Almighty. The *tallit*, however, is more than a mere vestment that adorns the worshipper. It is the Jew's literal fulfillment of one of God's specific commandments in the Holy Scriptures. It is also a living emblem to the Jewish people, a symbol that speaks to them of their faith in the *one* God of the Bible and their devotion to his precepts and commandments.

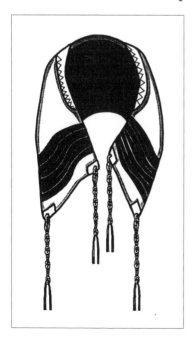

THE TALLIT OF ANCIENT TIMES

From the giving of the law at Sinai, the *tallit* had certain identifying characteristics that set the Jewish people apart as being chosen of God. What made it uniquely characteristic of the Jews was the fact that God required his chosen people to append one *tzitzit* (tassel) in each of the four corners of their outer garments. This is Torah's commandment: "Speak unto the children of Israel, and bid them that they make them fringes in the borders [corners] of their garments throughout their generations, and that they put upon the fringe of the borders a ribband of blue: and it shall be unto you for a fringe, that ye may look upon it, and remember all the commandments of the Lord, and do them; and that ye seek not after your own heart and your own eyes, after which ye use to go a whoring: that ye may remember, and do all my commandments, and be holy unto your God" (Numbers 15:38-40). This commandment is reiterated in the Fifth Book of Moses in a more concise form and without added explanation: "Make tassels on the four corners of the cloak you wear" (Deuteronomy 22:12). The specific reason for this command was that the *tzitzit* would be a visible symbol to direct the wearer's attention to God's commandments so that he would seek God's heart and not his own ways.

Initially, the *tallit* was not an extra vestment. It was merely the outer four-cornered garment to which the *tzitziyot* were appended. According to Jewish tradition, this garment had to be a hand's breadth shorter in length than the garment under it. The inner garment was a tunic (called *haluk* in Hebrew) and could be worn in the home or when one was engaged in physical activity where the outer robe would be too cumbersome.

During the Babylonian captivity, the Jewish people began to adopt the fashions of their Gentile neighbors. This was particularly true of those who chose to remain outside Israel following the exile. Such conformity to popular styles of dress was not unusual, however, for the Jews had always assimilated garment designs from their neighbors, simply adapting *tzitziyot* to the fashions of the day.

After the time of Alexander the Great, Greek attire became the social norm throughout the Seleucid Empire and Greater Persia.

As time progressed, many of the Jewish people found themselves wearing clothing that had no distinctive corners to which they could attach fringes; therefore, the traditional *tallit* gradually faded into disuse. Anxious to fulfill the commandments, however, the Jews decided to retain the robe, not as a main garment, but as a shawl or surplice worn as a religious garment: the prayer shawl. The name *tallit* was maintained throughout the centuries for this liturgical garment. By wearing this surplice during the day, the Jewish people could continue to wear the *tzitzit*, which were essential to fulfilling the commandment. Again, as fashions changed and the wearing of a fringed surplice became an incongruity, the Jewish people came to wear the *tallit* only for prayer, in both home and synagogue.

Until well after the destruction of the temple and the Roman occupation, the Jews in Israel continued to wear the *tallit* as a simple outer garment with *tzitziyot* attached in the four corners. The transition from *tallit* and *tzitzit* that were worn throughout the day to *tallit* as a prayer shawl was not complete even for Jews in the Diaspora until centuries later. The modern "prayer shawl" is more recent, dating to the time of Medieval Europe. Obviously, the

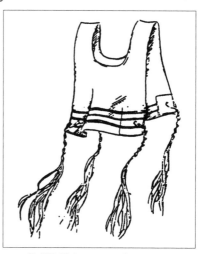

Tallit Katan **worn by many Jewish men**

prayer shawl was not the original intent of the *mitzvah*, for the *tzitziyot* were to remind the Jews of the commandments at all times, requiring that they be worn at all times. At an early period, the answer for many Jews was to devise a "*tallit katan*," a miniature *tallit* complete with fringes that could be worn under the outer garments. This garment, also called "*arba kanfot*" (four corners), is a rectangular piece of cloth made of linen, silk, or wool with an aperture in the center through which the head can pass. It has the four essential corners to which the *tzitziyot* are attached. Orthodox males wear the *tallit katan* from the age of three throughout their lives.

UNIQUENESS OF ISRAEL'S TALLIT

Until this time, clothing for mankind had served only as a reminder of the sin of Adam and Eve when they rebelled against the one commandment that God had enjoined upon them. Indeed, the Hebrew word for garment (usually the outer garment or *tallit*) is *beged*, which is derived from the root *bagad*, meaning to rebel or to be faithless. Perhaps God had allowed the garment that he gave to cover man's nakedness to serve as a continuing reminder of his rebellion. Now, however, God took the symbol of sin and death and made it a reminder that he had set before Israel a choice between life and death, between a blessing and a curse. The opportunity for life was found in faith toward God and obedience of his commandments that were vividly impressed upon their memories by the *tzitziyot* that were now to be appended to the four corners of their garments.

A loving God designed a system of reminders to assist his chosen people in remembering his commandments and expressing their love to him: he provided visible markings in their clothing and elsewhere that constantly summoned them to obedience to his Word. This practice was no burden to the Jewish people but a privilege, a badge of honor through which they could visibly demonstrate their commitment to the Word of God.

Following God's commandments and the leading of his Spirit involves complete submission to the divine will, a total dependence upon God. The fringes that God requires his people to attach to their garments remind them not only of his commandments but also that they are not to live their lives after their own ways. Theirs are to be lives not only of obedience but also of trust, not only of submission but also of living faith.

THE TALLIT IN JESUS' TIME

Due to the gradual change in the style and manner of fulfilling the commandment of *tzitzit*, we cannot know the exact state of the *tallit* in Jesus' day with absolute certainty. We can be sure, however, that it was not the prayer shawl of modern times. Misunderstanding this historical fact, the *New International Version* mistranslates Matthew 23:5: "They make . . . the tassels of their *prayer shawls* long." In the days of Jesus, the *tallit* had not yet become the modern praying surplice, used at the time of morning prayer. It was still an outer garment, like the Hellenic toga, worn throughout the day when one was in public. Incidentally, it is quite ironic that, while the *New International Version* translates the Greek words *kraspedon . . . himation* as "tassels of their prayer shawls" when referring to Jews and hypocrisy in Matthew 23:5, it translates precisely the same phrase as "the hem of his garment" when it refers to Jesus and the miraculous healing in Matthew 9:20.

Since Jesus was a faithful, Torah-observant Jew, he fulfilled God's commandment to wrap himself in the *tallit*. To the general public, both from Israel and from the nations round about, he was immediately recognized as a Jew by the flowing tassels that were attached to his *tallit*. Like all observant Jewish males of his day, he was a walking reminder that God's people were to remember all his commandments and observe them.

A DISTINCTIVE BLUE THREAD

Literally and grammatically there was something more about the *tzitzit* that was to call Israel's attention to the commandments of God. In each *tzitzit* was to be a single ribband (thread) of blue. Even more than the *tzitzit* itself, this single blue thread was to be the reminder of God's *mitzvot*. Gramatically, the antecedent of the pronoun *it* in the text (upon which Israelites were to look and remember) is "ribband" or the thread of blue (*tekhelet* in Hebrew). The *tekhelet* thread was to be exactly the same color as the high priest's robe, which was "all of blue." The other elements of the high priest's garments were decorated with blue as well as with gold, purple, and scarlet. The official uniform, then, in which the high priest approached the service of the Tabernacle was "all of *tekhelet*" with various other accents. This fact is very important when one considers its implications when applied to each Jewish man's *tallit*.

The *tzitzit* was constructed of seven white strands of thread (a symbol of purity and perfection) entwined with the one blue thread, called the *shamash* or servant thread. The total of eight threads in the *tzitzit* manifests the number of new beginnings. White is also the symbol of forgiveness and atonement (Isaiah 1:18). God, himself, is covered in white: "Who coverest thyself with light as with a garment . . . His raiment was white as snow" (Psalm 104:2; Daniel 7:9). Blue is the color of truth. The blue thread was the completion of the *tallit* and its *tzitziyot*. Its striking blue demanded the attention of its observer to the uniqueness of the fringe and to its avowed purpose of emphasizing God's commandments.

In the time of Jesus, the *tallit* with *tzitzit* with a thread of *tekhelet* was most certainly in use by Jewish men. It is likely that by that time an updated form of the ancient mantle was in popular use, perhaps even a precursor of the modern prayer shawl. At any rate, there can be no doubt but that the garment which Jesus wore as an integral part of his Torah-centric lifestyle was the *tallit* with *tzitzit* and *tekhelet*. His mantle was a rectangular woolen garment with a fringe appended and hanging down from each of its four corners. This was the "hem" of his garment which brought healing to "all who touched it."

WHY TZITZIT

Considering the exorbitant cost of the ancient blue dye, why would God require every Israeli male to display a thread of this blue in each corner of his mantle? Considering the difficulty of constructing fringes and attaching them to the outer garment, why would God consider it important for his people to make such a display? The *tzitziyot* are not essential to the structural integrity of the garment.

Perhaps one reason that God made this requirement was to emphasize the fact that every man in Israel as the head of a family had the responsibility of being both king and priest in his home. He was to lead his family in worship of God and in the priestly act of extending God's providential blessings upon both his wife and children, the same blessings that God had instructed Aaron to place upon all the children of Israel. When any Jew saw the blue thread in his *tzitzit*, he was immediately reminded that he was a part of that "kingdom of priests" that God had uniquely called unto himself. The Israelites were commanded to place a blue thread in the *tzitziyot* of their *tallit* because they understood themselves to be *banim la-Makom*, noble sons of the King of the universe, always pursuing God's commandments, an understanding that remains to this day.

The second reason for the *tzitzit* was so that "ye may look upon it, and remember all the commandments of the Lord, and do them." Both the *tzitzit* and the *tekhelet* are physical reminders of all the commandments of God, encouraging Jews to "do them." This call to remembrance and observance of the commandments is manifest in the *tzitzit* of the *tallit* on three different levels, first with the *Shema* (the greatest commandment), then with the Decalogue (Ten Commandments), and finally with the total of all the commandments (*mitzvot*).

The most important commandment in the entire Word of God is the *Shema*: "Hear, O Israel, the Lord our God, the Lord is One: and thou shalt love the Lord thy God with all thy heart, and with all thy soul, and with all thy mind, and with all thy strength." Jesus confirmed the fact that this was the first and greatest commandment (Matthew 22:38).

The *Shema's* most important declaration is: "The Lord is One." In Hebrew, this phrase is "*Y-H-W-H Echad*." Each letter in the Hebrew alphabet has a numerical equivalent, so that *aleph* (a) is 1, *beth* (b) is 2, *gimmel* (g) is 3, and so forth. When the corresponding numbers for the Hebrew letters in *Y-H-W-H* are added, the sum is 26; therefore, *Y-H-W-H* numerically equals 26. When the corresponding numbers for *echad* are added, the sum is 13.

These numbers (and their corresponding Hebrew words) are seen in the *tzitzit* in the following manner: the *tzitzit* has five double knots (corresponding to the Pentateuch, the five books of Moses) with four sets of wrappings between them. The first three sets of wrappings total 26 (set one: 7 wrappings; set two: 8 wrappings; set three: 11 wrappings). Twenty-six is the numerical equivalent of God's own personal name (*Y-H-W-H*). Then, the fourth set of wrappings totals 13, the numerical equivalent of *echad*, "one." When an observant Jew, then, looks upon the *tzitzit* of his prayer shawl, he first sees the numbers 26 and 13, which correspond precisely to *Y-H-W-H Echad* ("the Lord is one"), the essential words of the greatest of all commandments, the *Shema*.

As a Jewish man looks upon the *tzitzit* of his *tallit*, he also sees the sum total of the *mitzvot*. Rashi explained how looking at the fringes reminds the Jewish man of all God's commandments, not just the Decalogue (as noted above). Again, using the fact that the letters of the Hebrew alphabet have numerical equivalents, Rashi demonstrated that the Hebrew word *tzitzit* is numerically equivalent to 600 and that the *tzitzit* is comprised of a total of 8 strings, tied with 5 knots, making a total of 13. When these numbers are added together, the sum is 613, the number of commandments in the Torah.

When an observant Jewish man looks upon and touches to his eyes the *tzitzit* of his *tallit*, he recognizes the *Shema* (the first and greatest commandment), the Ten Commandments, and the 613 *mitzvot*. Furthermore, he is constantly reminded to do them, submitting himself to the will of God.

THE HEM OF JESUS' GARMENT

Jesus was a believing, practicing Jew who fully observed the heritage in which he had been trained by his parents. They "did everything according to the law of Moses," the Scripture tells us (Luke 2:39). Jesus was a Jew, and the religion that he observed throughout his lifetime was Biblical Judaism, "the Way of the Torah." He was bold and unequivocal: "We know what we worship: for salvation is from the Jews," he declared (John 4:22).

Because Jesus was an observant Jew, he dressed and groomed himself in accordance with the commandments of the Torah. He wore the fringed mantle, having *tzitziyot* on the four corners of his outer garment. When the woman with the issue of blood and the people of Gennesaret "touched the hem of his garment," they were not grasping the broad band at the edge of some sumptuous robe. They were touching the *tzitzit* on the corners of the Master's *tallit*. It might well have been an act of their faith that Jesus was the fulfillment of the promise in Malachi 4:2: ". . . the Sun of righteousness will arise with healing in his wings." The word translated "wings" in this prophecy is *kanaph*, which means corner, the exact part of the mantle where the *tzitziyot* were attached.

The *tzitziyot* had come to symbolize authority among the Jewish people (cf. Saul's ripping the *tzitzit* from Samuel's mantle and David's cutting the *tzitzit* from Saul's cloak). They had also come to symbolize all the commandments or the very Word of God. In effect, then, those who reached out to touch the "hem" of Jesus' garment were grasping the visible object that symbolized God's Word. They were claiming the promise that God "healeth all thy diseases" (Psalm 103:3).

This is proof positive that Jesus was a fully observant Jew, fulfilling all the commandments of God's Word in complete continuity with the faith of his ancestors. Though the truth has been obscured by inadequate translation of the accounts of these miracles, the historical and theological truth remains: Jesus wore the fringed garment as did all of his brethren "according to the flesh."

A RICH TRADITION

The wearing of *tzitziyot* attached to the four corners of the outer garment (whether the ancient mantle or the more modern prayer shawl) is a rich tradition of devotion to the specific details of a divine commandment. One must remember that this practice is the result of divine imperative, not of man's invention: it is God's commandment to his people, not their scheme to secure or maintain his attention.

For those who know nothing of the biblical basis for the *tallit* and *tzitzit* and for the Jewish literalist interpretation of the commandment and tradition that surrounds its continuing use, the practice may seem quaint and anachronistic. Indeed, many modern Jews regard the *tallit* tradition in this manner. For those who make it a part of their daily devotion to God and his Word, however, it is rich in meaning.

Before putting on the four-cornered garment, Jewish men for some nineteen centuries have recited the following benediction: "Blessed art thou, O Lord our God, King of the universe, who has sanctified us by thy commandments, and has commanded us to wrap ourselves in *tzitzit*." While it is believed that this benediction dates to the Tannaic period after the destruction of the temple, it is possible that Jesus recited some form of it. Today, this same benediction is embroidered on the *atarah* (crown) of most prayer shawls so that a man may see the blessing as he recites it.

In modern times, the *tallit* is worn each day during the morning prayers (*Shacharit*), except on the Ninth of Av, when it is worn at the afternoon service, and on *Yom Kippur* (the Day of Atonement), when it is worn all day. The *tallit* is worn only during the day because the biblical commandment specifies that the *tzitzit* must be *seen*. In fact, the evening *Kol Nidrei* service on *Yom Kippur* begins before sunset, so that a Jew can wrap himself in his *tallit* while he can still see the *tzitziyot*.

Immediately after the recitation of the blessing, the *tallit* is put on, covering the head first. Then, the four corners are thrown over the left shoulder, a movement called 'atifat Yishma'elim ("after the manner of the Ishmaelites, or Arabs"). After a short pause, the four corners are then al-

lowed to fall back into their original position, two sus-
pended on both sides of the worshipper. Strictly observant Jews pray with the *tallit* covering their head, believing
that to be enfolded by the *tallit* is to be enveloped by the
holiness of the commandments of the Torah, denoting symbolic subjection to the divine will. It is also customary in
the morning service to press the *tzitzit* to the eyes and to
kiss them three times during the recital of the final section
of the *Shema* that deals with the commandment of the
tzitzit. As a praying mantle, the *tallit* expresses and
conduces to a spirit of sublime devotion and consecrated
meditation, inspiring in the heart a feeling of awe and reverence. A token of the honor that the *tallit* is accorded is
seen in the fact that whenever Torah scrolls are moved,
they are generally covered in a *tallit* to protect them.

The *tallit* stands on solid biblical ground as a means
of drawing the Jewish worshipper to attention so that he
remembers the commandments of God and enters with
kavanah (intensity and devotion) into his time of prayer
for passionate, intimate relationship with God. Bible-believing Christians would do well to respect this tradition
and the piety of the Jewish people who observe it in honor
of God.

CHRISTIANS AND TALLIT

Objects of honor from one faith should not be ex-
ploited or abused by those of another. Christians should
be careful to honor the importance of the *tallit* tradition
for the Jewish community by not misusing or expropriating the *tallit* for their own purposes. Some use these and
other accoutrements of Judaism to make themselves appear Jewish in order to gain some advantage in "witness-
ing" to Jewish people, thinking that somehow the end
justifies the means. Such abuse and deception is unethical
and should not even be considered, much less practiced

among Christians. Others employ Jewish articles in an effort to inflate their own estimation of themselves as somehow being "Jewish." Wearing Jewish liturgical garments and displaying Jewish artifacts do not make one Jewish any more than donning a robe and a white wig makes one a British magistrate.

A growing number of Christians make such use of traditionally Jewish articles in an effort to identify with the Jewish people and to demonstrate understanding that their Christian faith is inherently Jewish. While such a desire for Christians to identify with the Jewish people is commendable, great care should be exercised not to misuse or misrepresent Jewish traditions. Christians who rush off to do Jewish things or to appear Jewish when they obviously know nothing of the subject are at best boorish and inconsiderate and at worst sacrilegious. We should remember that sensitivity is the Golden Rule in action.

Great lessons about the Jewishness of Jesus and the apostles can be learned from the articles that they most certainly used in their own worship of God. Every material article–like every spiritual exercise–that was patterned and modeled on the Hebrew Scriptures can be found in some way to point to the Messiah. Both Jesus and Paul declared this to be the fundamental purpose of the Torah. Truths that are profoundly enhancing to Christian faith are readily discernible in Judaism and Jewish practices. Metaphors and allegories can be legitimately drawn from these sources in the same manner in which the New Testament writers did; however, care should be exercised when doing so to ensure that they are set in the context of the grammar and historico-cultural setting in which they were employed by the earliest church.

While Christians can certainly learn rich lessons about their Jewish Lord from the *tallit* tradition, they are not required to wear one when they pray. Indeed, the fulfillment of the command establishing *tzitzit* as a means of remembrance of God's commandments should be manifest in a fully biblical lifestyle of walking in the Holy Spirit and letting the light of God's Messiah shine through one's good works of obedience to God's Word. Christian believers who fully experience the living Christ are not merely enveloped in the Torah, they are endued with the living Torah through the indwelling lawgiver, the Holy Spirit.

It is unlikely that pious, Torah-observant Jews would begrudge Christians the legitimate, respectful use of any Jewish artifact that would draw a believer closer to God and his Word in pure, sincere devotion. If wearing a prayer shawl during times of prayer helps one to focus on and interact with the Divine, one could profit from such. If one is convicted by the Holy Spirit (not by one's own soulish impulses) that he should practice Jewish things, such an exercise is legitimate and is birthed in freedom. They are certainly of value and are analogous to various material practices in Christian churches that are designed to focus the worshipper's attention on God and his service. If ministers wish to use a *tallit* as a vestment or if churches wish to use it as a parament in their sanctuaries at significant times to affirm their identity with the Jewish people, such use is appropriate.

A classic example of the depth that is added to the Christian experience by understanding the Hebraic matrix from which Christianity emerged is the *tallit* tradition of biblical, Second Temple, and rabbinic Judaism. As we have seen, this tradition impacted the lives of prophets, kings, and ancestors of the Messiah in the Hebrew Scriptures and of Jesus, his disciples, and the people to whom they ministered.

Without an understanding of this rich biblical tradition from the Judaic heritage of Christian faith, we have an incomplete view of what actually happened in Jesus' ministry. We are left to draw our own conclusions based on our own cultures and traditions. With this background of the circumstances that were the context of New Testament events, we share a richness that expands our understanding and invigorates our faith. And this is but one small element in the vast treasure house of riches that awaits those who search diligently to discover the Hebraic truths that often lie just beneath the surface of our Bible translations. Understanding the Hebrew foundations of our Christian faith is, indeed, a golden key that unlocks the treasures of Holy Scripture for those who passionately pursue the truths of God's living, infinite, immutable Word.

Chapter 6

The
Tefillin

Perhaps one of the most quaint of the external symbols that are used in Jewish worship is *tefillin*, the leather boxes that are worn on the arm and on the forehead by Jewish men during morning prayers. These are totally unique in modern practice and seem anachronistic, even incongruous with modern dress and modes of worship. Through the history of the Jews, rabbinic tradition has elaborately developed this practice; however, this sacred symbol is solidly based on the words of Holy Scripture. While not all Jews use *tefillin*, these sacred symbols have been profoundly significant in Judaism.

A TORAH COMMANDMENT

The Torah specifically gave Israel this command: "Therefore shall ye lay up these my words in your heart and in your soul, and bind them for a sign upon your hand,

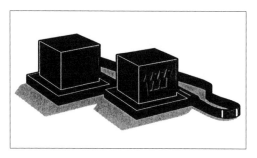

that they may be as frontlets between your eyes" (Deuteronomy 11:18). Though many have considered this commandment merely symbolic of the fact that whatever one does with his hands and whatever he understands with his mind must be that which God has ordained in his Word, Jewish tradition is not content with simply "spiritualizing" these passages. Rather, it gives concrete expression to one's personal commitment to these lofty concepts by literally carrying them out. This should not be understood as mere slavish devotion to the letter of the law but as a living adjunct to a life of commitment to these sublime principles.

Because this Torah passage mentions two places where God's Word is to be displayed, there are two *tefillin*. These are black leather boxes (at least one cubic inch in size) sewn together as a cube by precisely twelve stitches. (Though the color black is normative for *tefillin*, in history any color could be used except blood red.) These boxes are then attached to leather straps of special design. With these black leather straps the *tefillin* are bound to the Jew's person during daily morning prayer services as a sign of God's covenant with the Jewish people. Jewish *aggadot* (folkloric legends based on the Bible) even suggest that God wears *tefillin* since he too is bound by the covenant with Israel.

What makes these boxes of consequence and a literal fulfillment of the Torah commandment is the fact that they contain small pieces of parchment on which are written four portions of the Torah, including the *Shema*: "Hear, O Israel, the Lord our God, the Lord is one." Jesus himself declared that the *Shema* is the first and most important commandment. The Scripture portions included in the *tefillin* are 1) the *Shema* (Deuteronomy 6:4-9), pronouncing the unity of the one God; 2) *Vehayah* (Deuteronomy 11:13-21), expressing God's assurance of reward to those who observe the precepts of Torah; 3) *Kadesh* (Exodus 13:1-10), underscoring the

duty of the Jewish people to remember their redemption from Egyptian bondage; and 4) a second *Vehayah*
(Exodus 13:11-16), reminding the Jew of his obligation
to inform his children of these matters.

The first passage contained in the *tefillin* declares that
God is one and that he is to be loved with every facet of
one's being. This establishes the fact that God is not an
abstraction of philosophy or mere force of nature, but
rather a personal Father to his people. The second passage
emphasizes that man's every thought and action must be
considered in the light of its results. The third passage underscores the responsibility that man has of making de-
finitive displays and actions of his faith. The fourth section
reminds Jewish worshippers that God has always been
present with them even in the most hopeless and devas-
tating times of their corporate existence. These four Torah portions are placed in both *tefillin*.

The *tefillin* for the hand has a single parchment scroll
on which the four passages of Scripture are written in
minute Hebrew characters. This is done because
Deuteronomy 11:18 declares that this *tefillin* is for a sign
(singular). The *tefillin* for the head has these passages written on four separate pieces of parchment, which, in turn,
are inserted in specific compartments within the box itself. This is done because this same passage states that
this *tefillin* is for "frontlets" (plural).

From the time that a Jewish male becomes *bar mitzvah*
at the age of thirteen, he is required to "lay" or put on
tefillin every weekday as a part of morning prayers, whether
in the home or synagogue. Because Sabbath and the festivals *per se* summon the Jew's attention to his faith, it is not
considered necessary that *tefillin* be worn on these occasions. Because they are considered to be an ornament, they
are also not worn in morning prayers on the fast of *Tisha
b'Av*, the national day of mourning in remembrance of the

destruction of the temple. They are worn instead in the afternoon service.

RICH SYMBOLISM

Rabbinic tradition has developed God's simple command into a system that makes it possible to bind the Word of God upon the hand and by extension to the arm so that it is positioned near the heart. This is with the *tefillin shel yad* (for the hand). The leather strap which is attached to this box is wrapped seven times around the left arm (right arm if the person is left handed), because the commandment says it is to be bound "upon thy hand [*yad*]," not "upon thy right hand [*yamin*]." It is then wound three times around the left hand and then three times around the middle finger of the hand, literally constructing the Hebrew letter *shin*, which stands for *El Shaddai*, one of the names of the Eternal God. In many communities, Hosea 2:21-22 is recited as one winds the leather strap around the middle finger. Wearing the *tefillin* on the arm indicates that the law of God is written upon one's heart. It is an outward demonstration of an inward reality. Does God want his law written literally on one's arm? Perhaps. Does he want it engraved in one's heart? Most definitely!

The *tefillin* that are worn on the head, the *tefillin shel rosh*, is a box identical to that worn on the arm, but it is attached to a strap designed in a circlet with a slip-knot that can be adjusted to fit one's head. This box is placed at the top of the forehead so that it is positioned at the hairline (before the seat of intelligence), where the kings of Israel were anointed. This is an outward demonstration of the inward reality that God's law is engraved in the worshipper's mind. It is also a graphic illustration that man's intelligence is under God's Word and, therefore, in submission to it.

Both the hand *tefillin* and the head *tefillin* fulfill in

literalist terms the commission recorded in Jeremiah 31:33 that the covenant of God's Torah should be written in one's heart and in his mind. The visible, material application of the commandment was never to be an end in itself. It was to underscore the importance of the spiritual reality that was to be a part of every Jew's existence. According to Hebrews 10:16, this very concept is the foundation of the new covenant that was manifest in Jesus. It was very simple for Jews to understand the new covenant in these terms, for it was not a different covenant but a renewed covenant, fully inscribing the terms of the Torah in the hearts and minds of the believers.

The name *tefillin* is derived from the Hebrew word for prayer, *pallal*. This ancient lexical root contains the idea of rolling something out flat, which is the essence of prayer, laying everything out in the presence of God to allow his Spirit to smooth out the rough places in life. It is through total submission of mind and heart to the will and Word of God that one is able to engage in prayer and worship. For the Jew, *tefillin* are visible, material symbols of what he purposes to do spiritually: submit the totality of his being (manifest through the heart and the mind) to God's commandments.

NEW TESTAMENT TEFILLIN

In the writings of the New Testament, *tefillin* were called phylacteries, from the Greek word for "protection." The idea for the use of this word in relationship to the *tefillin* is that one who is continually reminded of his duty to be subject in heart and mind to the Word of God is fully protected from sin and disobedience. Maimonides stressed the protection of the observant Jew: "The holiness of the *tefillin* is great, for so long as the *tefillin* are upon the head and the arm of a man, he is humble and God-fearing, keeps away from levity and idle talk, does not conceive evil thoughts, and turns his heart exclusively to words of truth and justice."

The pagan Greeks perceived the *tefillin* as mere amulets worn by the Jewish people in an effort to ward off evil spirits. It is doubtful that the Jews themselves ever subscribed to this notion, for the vast majority of Jews would have considered the idea repugnant and even blasphemous. The *tefillin* were designed not to protect from evil spirits but to remind their wearers of their ethical responsibility to remember and do all the commandments of God's Word.

One should no more consider the laying of *tefillin* a superstitious act than to suggest that the wearing of a clerical collar or other vestment is the same. These Christian symbols are worn to indicate one's calling as a person set apart to God's service and as perpetual reminders to their wearers that they have come under the yoke of Christ's leadership and are consecrated to him in lives of holiness and service. Likewise, *tefillin* must be recognized as living emblems of the Jewish people's faith that is focused solely upon the one God and upon the commandments of his Word.

Others have taken the lone mention of *tefillin* (phylacteries) in the New Testament to indicate that their use is always an ostentatious show of one's self righteousness. Wearing *tefillin* is also said to be contrary to the justification by faith that Jesus and the apostles taught. Indeed, Jesus did upbraid some of his fellow Jews for their hypocrisy with these words: "Everything they do is done for men to see: They make their phylacteries wide and the tassels of their prayer shawls long . . ." (Matthew 23:5). Since there was no specific instruction in Torah regarding the size of *tefillin* or the *tzitzit* of the *tallit*, some Jews did make their displays large and bold, thinking that thereby they could impress their fellow Jews with the degree of their piety. This did not, however, characterize the vast majority of the Pharisees and other sects of Jews.

Jesus was not condemning the practice of wearing *tefillin* or *tzitzit*. He was addressing the hypocrisy of making ostentatious displays in order to impress men. This is certainly a characteristic that can find many modes of manifestation among Christians as well as among Jews. Some Christians who think that somehow their piety is demonstrated by the size and beauty of their accoutrements are no different than their Jewish counterparts whom Jesus challenged.

It is likely that Jesus himself wore *tefillin* as an outward demonstration that was very much a part of the Judaism which he practiced. Since it was said of him that he knew no sin, it is certain that he did not violate any of the Torah commandments, for we are specifically told that "sin is the transgression of the law" (1 John 3:4). While Jesus himself may not have adopted such a literalist interpretation of the passage requiring that the law be bound to the hand and worn on the forehead, he likely accommodated this outward traditional manifestation to remain in continuity with the faith of his fathers. It is certain that Jesus was readily distinguishable as a Jew (cf. the account of the woman at the well of Samaria in John 4). In Jesus' time *tefillin* were likely worn at all times, just as the *tallit* with its *tzitzit* was worn throughout the day and was not merely a prayer shawl. Though the size and shape of the *tefillin* may well have been somewhat different from what

How *Tefillin* are bound to the arm and forehead

are now worn by the Jewish people, those found with the Dead Sea Scrolls testify to the ongoing continuity of Jewish tradition. Whatever the case may have been, Jesus is likely to have participated in this tradition.

CHRISTIANS AND TEFILLIN

What should be the Christian position toward the laying of *tefillin*? While most believers will take the commandment in a figurative rather than a literal sense, as do the Karaite Jews to this day, some may be convicted that it is important to make a literal, physical display of their submission to the Word of God. Since there is no specific biblical commandment as to the design or wearing of *tefillin*, one may choose to employ what the rabbis have approved.

A believer is under no injunction, however, to practice this outward demonstration as the Jewish people are convicted to do. If he chooses to make such a demonstration, of whatever sort, he must do so by personal conviction and not by constraint from the expectations of others. Anyone who is convicted to engage in such a practice, moreover, must be careful that he not be exalted in his own eyes to a level of self-righteousness and hypocrisy that will manifest itself in judgmentalism directed against those who are not similarly convicted. Whatever one does or does not do must be done as unto the Lord. This flexibility is grounded in Paul's teaching of pluriformity (not uniformity), which the apostle learned at the feet of Gamliel and in the school of the great Hillel. (Romans 14 contains a magnificent example of this apostolic flexibility that permitted Paul to "become all things to all men.")

LIVING EMBLEMS

To the observant Jew, *tefillin* are indeed living emblems, ancient symbols of faith. They function like spiritual armor, protecting the Jew from sin and evil thought because they serve as reminders of the worshipper's obligation to remember all of God's words and do them. For the Jew, then, the laying of *tefillin* is considered a sacred privilege, not a cumbersome obligation. Like David of old, they choose to "delight" in the law of God (Psalm 119:47, 70). Though quaint in appearance to the modern world, this material demonstration underscores the Jew's faith in the living God and in the authority of his Word upon his life.

Chapter 7
The
Kiddush Cup

The *Kiddush* cup is a prominent symbol in Judaism, not so much for the cup itself as for the blessing that is pronounced in honor of the Sabbath or festival when one partakes of the cup. It is also one of the clearest examples of objects and practices in Judaism that were carried over into Christianity, used first by Jesus and the apostles and then by millions of Christians through the centuries. The cup of blessing is a sacred symbol *par excellence*.

Kiddush means "sanctification" and is applied to the ceremony in which the goblet is used to introduce and set apart various occasions in Judaism. Originally, it was used to inaugurate the family *Shabbat* (Sabbath) and festival services as well as to formalize the conclusion of the family Sabbath service (*havdalah*). In Ashkenazic services it came to be used as well in a congregational *Kiddush*. No food or drink may be consumed on *Shabbat* or festivals until *Kiddush* has been

recited.

Because so many of Judaism's worship experiences are centered in family interaction and take place around the table, it is not unusual for items of food and drink to be used to call attention to the Divine and to extend worship and honor to him. The *Kiddush* cup contains wine, the natural essence of the grape. A universal symbol of joy, wine is used to call attention to the fact that God himself is the source of joy for the Jewish people and that the joy of the Lord is their strength (Nehemiah 8:10).

At the beginning of the Sabbath, at several times during Passover, and at other occasions the cup of wine is lifted in honor of the God of Israel who is blessed with the following benediction: "*Baruch atah, Adonai Elohenu, Melekh haOlam, boreh pri hagafen*" ("Blessed are you, O Lord our God, King of the universe, who creates the fruit of the vine"). This benediction is often accompanied by a similar blessing that is repeated over the bread: "*Baruch atah, Adonai Elohenu, Melekh haOlam, hamotzi lechem min ha'aretz*" ("Blessed are you, O Lord our God, King of the universe, who brings forth bread from the earth").

THE CUP OF BLESSING

The use of wine in blessing God and man is an ancient practice. It was manifest in Melchizedek's blessing of Abraham some four millennia ago: "And Melchizedek king of Salem brought forth bread and wine: and he *was* the priest of the most high God" (Genesis 14:18). In this case, the priest-king of Salem blessed Abraham, but he also blessed the Lord for giving the patriarch the victory which he was celebrating by bringing the tithe to the man of God. And, in the process of the blessing, Melchizedek brought forth "bread and wine."

It is likely that the use of the cup in blessing God and man was a long-standing practice–it certainly was manifest in the life of the first Hebrew. Because Abraham was blessed in his special relationship with God, all of his progeny have also been blessed. God himself promised, "I will bless them that bless thee" (Genesis 12:3). Indeed, Abraham was proclaimed to be a source of blessing to all the "families of the earth." Each time a believer in the God of Abraham, Isaac, and Jacob raises the cup and declares, "Blessed are you, O Lord our God, King of the universe," he is reenacting what Melchizedek did in blessing God when he also blessed Abraham.

This is what also occurs in the lives of those who have come to faith in God through Jesus as Messiah and Lord. They have been given the joy of the Holy Spirit instead of the spirit of heaviness forced upon them by their sin. When they participate at the Lord's table, they likewise lift the cup in blessing to the One who has given them life and righteousness, and they discern in the fruit of the vine the blood of the new covenant that has extended the blessing of Abraham to all the nations of the world through the promised Son by engraving God's commandments on the hearts of believers (Jeremiah 31:31-33; Hebrews 8:8-10).

This is the thrust of Paul's declaration concerning the communion: "The cup of blessing which we bless, is it not the communion of the blood of Christ?" (1 Corinthians 10:16). The "cup of blessing" was the *Kiddush* cup, and to the earliest Christians (as well as to all subsequent believers), it was a sharing (*koinonia*) of the blood of the new covenant. Because Christ our Passover has been sacrificed for us, we observe the festival that most frequently employs the *Kiddush* cup, Passover (1 Corinthians 5:8). Believers celebrate the communion more frequently than Passover, however, because the cup of blessing was and is raised each Sabbath in observant Jewish homes. The cup that Jesus used to institute communion at the Last Supper was the third of four cups used in the Passover *seder* of his time: the "cup of redemption." It is, however, the same cup that is elevated in honor of God each Sabbath–the *Kiddush* cup.

In reality, the practice instituted by Jesus should be confirmed in the context of the family each Sabbath. When the family comes together in the time set apart for blessing and worship in the home, the cup should be lifted in honor of the One who shed his blood that all might live. While the celebration of communion in the context of community in a public demonstration was clearly a practice of the earliest church, there is no hint of apostolic prohibitions against the ongoing practice of sanctifying the home worship experience by giving the ancient blessing with the bread and wine.

BLESSING GOD

The blessings of Judaism are always extended to God himself, never to the object that is to be used in worship. In Jewish thought, there is no need for one to bless the wine, the bread, or any other material object, for everything material is considered to be blessed already, having been created by God himself and pronounced "good" at its first formation (Genesis 4:31). The concept of blessing the wine and bread in Christian communion is a result of the Christianity's Hellenization and Latinization in which concepts derived from Gnosticism and neo-Platonism infiltrated the church's doctrine and polity. Because many of the Greek philosophers considered matter *per se* to be evil, the need to "bless" various material substances so that they could be put to "holy" use became a dominant theme in the post-Nicene and medieval church. Hence the practice of "blessing" the wine and bread of communion by the spoken word of a recognized priestly authority.

When the wine or bread was "blessed," it became holy,

and even its substance ultimately was considered to have been altered. One of the tragic results of the incursion of this Greek concept into the life of the Christian community was the emergence of a priestly class, who were thought to have been elevated to a higher state of holiness and were, therefore, separated from the "laity" of the church. The mystical action involved in blessing matter served to reinforce the power of the clergy over the laity and produced the clergy-laity gap from which the church has never recovered. It also served as a basis for Christianity's concept of sin's being inherent in various material objects and in bodily functions. This confusion produced guilt and the attendant need for expiation, further reinforcing the power of the church through its professional priesthood.

Practices that had been carried out in every Jewish home by the head of each household were taken from that context and reserved to professional clergymen. This destroyed the head of household's role as priest in the home in simple worship experiences that honored God in the context of family, and it reserved that role as the province of an exalted few. Christianity, therefore, became predominantly a spectator-based religion rather than the participatory faith originally intended.

Even Holy Scripture was interpolated and mistranslated to reflect this idea from Greco-Roman dualism that required the "blessing" of material objects so as to make them fit for "holy" use. The King James Version reflects this interpolation in its translation of Matthew 26:26: "And as they were eating, Jesus took bread, and blessed *it*, and brake *it*, and gave *it* to the disciples, and said, Take, eat; this is my body." In each case here, "it" is italicized to indicate that the word is not in the original text. The interpolation, however, paints the indelible picture that Jesus blessed *the bread*. Luke 24:30 also reflects this interpolation, which is based in church tradition and general ignorance of Judaism, the religion that Jesus practiced. The truth is that Jesus blessed *God* for bringing forth bread from the earth just as every other Jew in his day would have done. The bread did not need to be blessed, for it was not evil. And his blessing did not change the substance of the bread so that it was no longer bread but his body. Though the disciples discerned in the bread the broken body of Jesus, the bread did not change substance.

Interestingly enough, when reference is made to Jesus' taking the cup, he is said to have given thanks (Matthew 26:27; Luke 22:17). This giving thanks before partaking of food was the act of benediction, blessing God for creating the fruit of the vine in the tradition of his forefathers. The Christian practice of "giving thanks" for food in advance of its consumption is derived from Second Temple Judaism in which the sages of Israel introduced the idea of blessing God for his provision of food and drink. The most ancient example of such worship was that God was blessed *after* the consumption of food: "When thou hast eaten and art full, then thou shalt bless the Lord thy God for the good land which he hath given thee" (Deuteronomy 8:10). The sages, however, felt it essential to bless God in advance of any action that brought pleasure or joy. Because Jesus and the apostles engaged in this practice of Second Temple Judaism, it was carried forward into the church. This is the thrust of Paul's statement regarding foods: "For every creature of God *is* good, and nothing to be refused, if it be received with thanksgiving" (1 Timothy 4:4).

This Pauline declaration has been used to reinforce the church's contention that material objects must be "blessed," for the apostle goes on to assert that the food is "sanctified by the word of God and prayer" (1 Timothy 4:5). Paul's use of the term *sanctification*, however, is in the context of the Jewish *Kiddush* tradition–that of sanctifying (setting apart) the occasion by the benediction (prayer). This statement did not enjoin upon the church Hellenism's idea of the inherent evil of material things. It does, however, confirm the clear truth that the church continued in the Hebraic heritage of Jesus in lifting the cup of blessing to honor God as the giver of joy and every spiritual and material benefit. The cup of blessing with which the early Christians blessed the Lord was the cup of salvation and sanctification. Through it, they set apart the most solemn and joyful event of their worship experience, the communion of the blood of Christ, and by it they also celebrated the salvation that had come to them by grace through faith in God's provision of redemption through Messiah.

CHRISTIANS AND THE KIDDUSH CUP

The *Kiddush* cup may be of any design. Generally, it is the finest, most highly decorated, or most expensive goblet used in the home. Since the cup of blessing was first used among the Jews in the context of the home Sabbath celebration, it is altogether appropriate that Christians make this a part of their family worship event. Since the contents of the cup need not be blessed (they are blessed already), there is no need for a specially ordained individual to "bless" the cup. The head of each household may either use the traditional Jewish formula for blessing God, devise a personal blessing, or give a spontaneous prayer that blesses God for his provision. It is also appropriate that family worship incorporate a blessing to God for bread. These elements may be shared by the priesthood of all believers in their individual homes to show forth their communion with Christ.

Corporate worship exercises should feature both the bread and the wine in celebration of the communion of the body and blood of the Messiah, for Christian believers were instructed by Jesus himself to "do this in remembrance" of his death until he returns. It is fitting that those who officiate on behalf of a congregation emphasize the ancient and continuing biblical tradition of the cup of blessing, underscoring the church's Jewish connection. In so doing, they help believers understand the continuity of biblical faith and the ancient basis for the practices they enjoy.

KIDDUSH: CELEBRATION AND EXPECTATION

Melchizedek brought forth bread and wine in that most ancient of celebrations. Subsequent generations of Hebrews have also lifted the cup in celebration of God as the giver of every good gift. Jews of all ages have initiated and sanctified God's holy days as times for family and God with the *Kiddish* cup. Jesus celebrated his last meal with his disciples by sharing bread and wine with them. Millions of Christian believers through the centuries have joined in communion with the living Lord by lifting up the cup of blessing. This represents a rich history of celebrating the cup of blessing.

Accompanying this celebration is a joyful expectation. The climactic event of the ages will be the coming of the Messiah and the accompanying age of peace. Jews expect the *coming* Messiah to restore the earth to the state of the Garden of Eden and to resurrect all the righteous dead to stand with him on Mount Zion. Christians expect the *returning* Messiah to establish God's dominion over all the earth and to empower the righteous to reign with him.

When that kingdom comes, our Lord has promised that he will renew the *Kiddush* cup tradition with his people (Matthew 26:29). No doubt, his elevation of the cup of blessing will initiate the greatest holy day of history, the Sabbatical Millennium of the kingdom of God.

Chapter 8

Passover Symbols

For the Jewish people, nothing in their history is more important than the deliverance of their ancestors from Egyptian slavery. Since the event that secured their freedom was the Passover, the circumstances of that historic night are memorialized in a yearly reenactment. Passover, therefore, is an essential annual festival for the Jewish people because it calls vividly to their remembrance the fact that they exist as an entity and are free from slavery because of the miraculous event that occurred in the lives of their ancestors some 3,500 years ago on this very day.

So important is the Passover to both the history and the present-day lives of the Jewish people that every Jew is required to think of himself as having been personally delivered from Egypt.

Passover, therefore, serves the function of providing a teaching forum in which the children of each family are instructed in this most important part of Israelite history. An indelible impression is made on the life of each Jewish child of observant homes that he (not just his ancestors) was delivered from Egyptian bondage by the outstretched arm of Israel's God.

DELIVERED FROM SLAVERY

The children of Israel had come to live in Egypt because Joseph, one of Jacob's twelve sons, had saved Egyptian society from a protracted famine of seven years' duration. They had been accorded status and privilege because the Pharaoh of that time had exalted Joseph to be second in command in the empire of Egypt. With the passing of time, however, a new Pharaoh arose "who knew not Joseph" (Exodus 1:8). When this occurred, the Egyptians, who owed their very existence to the spiritual insight that the Israelite patriarch had received from God to save their civilization from decimation, began to look upon the Israelites as servants who could be forced to do their bidding.

The enslavement grew in nature and scope until finally the Israelites were treated virtually as animals with no human rights. They were forced to construct many of the magnificent structures that were a part of the Pharaohs' obsession with their status in the afterlife. As their tasks became progressively more difficult and their lives became increasingly more unbearable, the Israelites cried out to God for deliverance. They knew that they were participants in the covenant that God had made with their father Abraham; therefore, they prayed to God in desperation for a deliverer who would rescue them from their oppression.

What they did not know was that at that very time,

the prophetic timepiece had reached the required position that had been predicted to Abraham when he was promised that his children would inherit the land of Israel. When he had received title to the land from the Euphrates to the River of Egypt by means of an irrevocable and inviolable covenant from the God who "cannot lie," Abraham had also been informed by God that his family would not possess the land for four hundred years (Genesis 15:13). Now that time had come.

God miraculously raised up Moses, placed him in the very household of the despot who had tried everything to destroy him (by attempting to kill all the Israelite male babies), and gave him the best education that was available anywhere in the world at that time. Then, God orchestrated the circumstances that brought Moses out of Egypt into the Sinai desert where he could prepare his heart for the fateful day when he would hear God's voice speaking to him from a burning bush and receive his commission to return to Egypt with this divine message for Pharaoh: "Let my people go."

Moses, the former prince of Egypt, returned as the prophet of God, faithfully delivering God's imperative to Pharaoh. God, however, hardened Pharaoh's heart so that rather than releasing the Israelite slaves, he escalated their oppression. Then, various plagues (a total of ten) were visited upon the land of Egypt in a manifestation of divine power that none in Egypt could match. Amazingly, Goshen, where the Israelites lived, was exempted from these plagues, each of which was directed against one of the gods of the Egyptians as well as against the Egyptian people. In each case, Pharaoh's heart was only further hardened.

Finally, God prepared to visit upon Egypt the tenth plague, which ironically took the form of the plan which Pharaoh had used in his attempt to destroy the anticipated

Israelite deliverer. The firstborn in every household in Egypt, including men and animals, was to be destroyed in one night of terror. In order to exempt Israel from this plague, however, God devised a special means, a process that he called "*pesach*" ("passover"). The Israelites were told that each family should kill a lamb at the entrance to their households and place the blood of that lamb on the doorposts and lintels of their homes. This would be a sign so that as God passed through Egypt, "when I see the blood, I will pass over you" (Exodus 12:13).

The children of Israel faithfully obeyed God's commandment through Moses and then waited within their homes, secure in the knowledge that they were protected by the blood of the lamb. The horrible outcries of grief that echoed throughout Egypt did not come from Israelite homes, for their firstborn were protected. When the plague reached even into Pharaoh's house, the hard-hearted most powerful man in the world relented and commanded the Israelites to leave his kingdom. On the following day, the Israelites left Egypt to begin their trek toward freedom and ultimately to a covenantal relationship with God as his chosen nation.

A COMMAND TO REMEMBER

Even before God delivered the Israelites from Egypt, he enjoined a specific commandment not only upon them but also upon all of their descendants: " . . . this day shall be unto you for a memorial; and ye shall keep it a feast to the Lord throughout your generations; ye shall keep it a feast by an ordinance for ever" (Exodus 12:14). Immediately after the people of Israel left their homes in Egypt, Moses reiterated God's requirement that they and their descendants annually celebrate this profound event.

This requirement was detailed in Leviticus 23, in the listing of Israel's liturgical calendar. It was repeated in various places throughout the Hebrew Scriptures as one of the three "Feasts of the Lord" that were to be celebrated in perpetuity by all the children of Israel. The chosen people were to remember continually that they had been delivered by God's outstretched arm, not by the diplomacy of their ancestors.

For nearly four millennia, therefore, the Jewish people have faithfully celebrated each anniversary of their liberation from Egypt with a memorial meal similar to the one their ancestors ate in haste that night when they were preparing for the exodus. Though the mode of expression for the meal may have changed over the centuries, the central elements have remained consistent. Each observant Jewish father has taught his children the lesson of God's deliverance at Passover.

PASSOVER UTENSILS

To facilitate the reenactment of the annual Passover memorial in each Jewish home, the sages of Israel have developed various utensils and other aids that accompany the celebration. These have become a part of an overall package of materials and information that makes it possible for each family, regardless of its level of knowledge, to join in the commemoration of Passover. Together they facilitate the Passover *seder* (order). Among these are the *Pesach* plate (or tray), the *matzoh* cover, the *Kiddush* cup, and the *Haggadah*.

In modern times, the one utensil that has become most helpful in the celebration is the *Pesach* plate, now known as *ke'arah* (platter) but formerly as *sal* (basket). Beautifully decorated, the *Pesach* plate is designed so that six of the major items of food that are featured on the Passover table are organized and remembered. This is important to the Jewish people because it arranges in order the elements of the Passover celebration that has been enjoined upon them forever. The *Pesach* plate features six circular indentations, one for each of the following foods: *maror* (bitter herbs, usually horseradish), *karpas* (parsley, celery, or boiled potatoes), *chazeret* (lettuce), *charoset* (a nut and apple mix), *zeroah* (the roasted lamb shankbone), and *beytzah* (a hard-boiled, roasted egg).

It is customary to arrange the plate in two triangles. The upper triangle, representing what was required in the Torah, has the shankbone on the right and the egg on the left. Neither the shankbone nor the egg is consumed in the ceremony because they represent respectively the Passover lamb and the attendant festival offering, the *chaggigah*, which can no longer be offered or consumed because the temple no longer exists. Then the *maror*, or bitter herbs, are placed in the center. The second triangle, representing rabbinic additions to the meal, is at the bottom of the platter and features the *charoset* on the right, the *karpas* on the left, and the lettuce in the center below them.

The *matzoh* cover features perhaps the most important part of the modern celebration of Passover, the unleavened bread with which the Israelites were commanded to remember the festival forever. It is the "bread of haste" which was prepared without time for leavening on the day of the exodus. For the seven days that follow, the Jewish people eat unleavened bread exclusively. The *matzoh* cover holds in three separate compartments, the three pieces of *matzoh* that are used during the *seder*. The three pieces symbolize for Jews the three divisions of the Hebrew Scriptures, the *Torah* (law), the *Nevi'im* (prophets), and the *Ketuvim* (writings). It is the middle piece that is broken and eaten, half with the *charoset* to remember the making of bricks in Egypt, and the other half as the *afikomen*, the dessert at the meal's conclusion.

The *Kiddush* cup is the cup of sanctification that is used to initiate or set apart each Sabbath day and each festival. It is used at the beginning of the *seder* as well as throughout the ceremony. Four cups of wine are poured and celebrated, remembering God's fourfold promise in Exodus 6:6: ". . . I will **bring you out** from under the burdens of the Egyptians, and I will **rid you out** of their bondage, and I will **redeem you** with a stretched out arm, and with great judgments; And I will **take you to me** for a people, and I will be to you a God: and ye shall know that I *am* the Lord your God, which bringeth you out from under the burdens of the Egyptians."

The *Haggadah* is a "story," a booklet that outlines the order of the ceremony for the one leading the *Pesach seder*. The name *Haggadah* is used in connection with the biblical injunction, "You shall instruct your son." There are many Passover *Haggadot* that offer beautiful readings for the various elements of the ceremony. By including all of the festival's essential elements, these *Haggadot* help the family enjoy a complete and proper Passover.

PASSOVER AND CHRISTIANS

Many Christians around the world have become convinced that some form of observance of God's festivals is important. Taking their cue from Paul's instruction to the Gentile believers at Corinth that they "observe the festival" of Unleavened Bread because "Christ our passover is sacrificed for us" (1 Corinthians 5:7), these believers are reclaiming festival observance as a part of their heritage as engrafted branches in God's family tree of salvation and covenantal relationship (Romans 11).

Christians can readily see in the Passover celebration many symbols that expand their understanding of the life and work of Jesus. For them, Passover is an opportunity to remember vividly the events that occurred on that day nearly 2,000 years ago when Jesus was crucified by Roman soldiers. It is a commemoration both of the deliverance of Israel from Egyptian bondage and the releasing of believers from slavery to sin through the One whom John called "the Lamb of God who takes away the sin of the world" (John 1:29 NIV).

While Christians can share in the celebration of the Passover, they should be careful that they respect the piety of the Jewish people who honor the day as they were instructed by God centuries ago. Christian celebrations must be seen not as supersessionist (employing "replacement theology") but as complementary to the historical Jewish celebrations. This is in keeping with the approach taken by the earliest church.

The Torah and its contingent celebrations were not destroyed by Jesus or the apostles. Their lives continued to revolve around the liturgical calendar of appointments that their ancestors had commemorated for centuries. They merely added their new-found understanding about the life, death, burial, resurrection, and ascension of Jesus to their already- existing system of praise, worship, and service. Gentile believers who were subsequently added to the church were considered to have become "fellow citizens" with the saints of Israel and naturalized citizens in the commonwealth or nation of Israel (Ephesians 2). As citizens of God's Israel, they had rights to the entitlements of citizenship. The same entitlements have been extended to all subsequent Christians.

Believers may wish to have the various elements of the Passover *seder* in their homes to be employed in a personal family remembrance of Passover or in an event for the collective, extended family. Such commemorations should be done with extreme honor for the ancient People of the Book and for their physical descendants. Those who have been awakened to the extensive harm that supersessionism has done to the Jewish people and to Jewish-Christian relations in history must not allow their dedication to the living Christ in their lives to cloud their vision and cause them merely to expropriate the sacred symbols of Judaism for their own purposes. In the tradition of Paul, who identified Christ as the Passover sacrifice, they may recognize the life and work of Jesus in the various elements of the Passover celebration; however, they must also recognize that these elements have profound significance to the Jewish people that is a part of their continuing participation in the Torah as God's instruction to them for worship of the Almighty.

Chapter 9

Sabbath Symbols

The Sabbath is the day that God set apart at the beginning of time when he himself rested from his labors of creation. The biblical record tells us that in six days God created the heavens and the earth and everything in them, and that he rested on the seventh day. In this action, the Creator established the principle that one-seventh of time should be set apart for rest, that one day in seven should be reserved for family and God.

A COMMANDMENT FOR MANKIND

When God gave the summation of his divine will to his newly chosen people at Sinai, he included one word

that reflected the importance of this principle of rest. "Remember the Sabbath day to keep it holy," he declared, noting that doing so would recall in the hearts of his people that their God had created everything that exists and that he had rested afterward. This was a simple mnemonic device to help God's people ascribe credit for existence and being to God and not to some evolutionary force.

In the second giving of the Ten Words, God noted to Israel that they should "keep the Sabbath" because they were slaves in Egypt and were delivered by God's hand. Since that time, the commemoration of the Sabbath has been one of the distinctive features of Judaism and the Jewish people. It has marked them apart from the rest of the world as a people separated unto God. Generation after generation has faithfully observed this memorial day each week, rejoicing in the Sabbath as a sanctuary in time set apart unto God.

Some have suggested that more important than the Jews' keeping the Sabbath has been the Sabbath's keeping the Jews, for this weekly time of devotion with family and God has been the single most important element in maintaining continuity in the Jewish home with the faith of their fathers. The sanctifying of time rather than places has preserved the Jewish connection to God and has accompanied the Jews wherever their forced wanderings have taken them. Dedicated to an invisible God through an intangible element (time), the perpetuation of their faith was not contingent upon spatial considerations. The Sabbath, not the temple or synagogue, maintained their continuing contact with the Divine and consequentially their *raison d'être*.

SACRED SYMBOLS

Several features are common to all Jewish observances of Sabbath, including festivals which are also Sabbaths. One of these is the ceremony of lighting the *Shabbat* candles in which at least two candles are lit before sundown on Friday to welcome the Sabbath. Some homes light one candle for each family member.

It is customary for the honor of welcoming *Shabbat* to be accorded to the women of the house. Though men are qualified to light the candles, the rabbis have admonished husbands against depriving their wives of this privilege. It is customary to light the candles at least eighteen minutes before sunset on Friday evening or the beginning of any festival. The biblical day begins at sundown, so that the evening precedes the morning (Genesis 1:5).

The wife first covers her head, then lights the Sabbath candles. She covers her eyes from seeing the light before pronouncing the benediction that sanctifies the Sabbath. After the benediction is given, the candles could not be lit, for with the benediction, the Sabbath/festival has officially begun, and a fire may not be lit on the Sabbath. In order to solve this dilemma, the wife covers her eyes from seeing the light while pronouncing the benediction so that symbolically at least, the sequence of benediction and performance is maintained.

Most Jewish homes have special *Shabbat* candlesticks that are reserved for this Friday evening celebration. These are often of great beauty, befitting the honor given to the holy day that God has prescribed for his people. They may be two or more candlesticks.

A second common element of the initiation of Sabbath/festival observance is the use of the *Kiddush* cup to sanctify or set apart the occasion of the Sabbath/Festival meals. In this part of the ceremony, the husband raises a special cup of wine and blesses God, "Blessed are you, O Lord our God, King of the universe, who has created the fruit of the vine." The *Kiddush* cup is a symbol of the joy of the Sabbath that permeates the hearts of all the family members.

A third element at the beginning of the Sabbath/festival meals is the benediction for bread. In this case, usually *challah* (a specially prepared bread) is used. *Challah* is Hebrew for "dough," but it is so called because of the woman's obligation to set aside the biblical portion of the dough for the priests (Numbers 15:18-21), a custom dating to the time of Jesus.

CHRISTIANS AND SHABBAT

Much of the church in history has considered Sunday to be the Christian Sabbath and has set apart this day for rest and worship. In effect, they have celebrated the principle of Sabbath if not the essence of the day. Today, more Christians are increasingly recognizing the importance of setting apart one day in seven, not just as a day to go to church, but as a time for celebration of God and family.

For Christians *Shabbat* can be a time of *remembering* (in the commandment's words): remembering God as Creator, remembering Jesus as the one who introduced an experience of salvation that allows believers to rest from their labors, secure in the completed work of Calvary, and remembering that in the coming Messianic Age both God and man will rest in the Millennial Kingdom of Christ.

Christians are free to engage in whatever practices bring richness, beauty, and joy to their worship experiences, both in the context of family and in corporate exercises. To honor with family devotions the day that God hallowed in the beginning and that Jesus certainly remembered throughout his lifetime is an opportunity for instruction in biblical truths about creation, re-creation, and the coming Messianic Age.

Whatever believers are convicted to do regarding the Sabbath are expressions that they should not force upon fellow believers. They have perfect liberty to worship God and to bring security and blessing to their families; however, they are not at liberty to judge others. As the Spirit of God brings more emphasis on restoration, the church will become more convicted about modes of expression that honor this part of God's appointment calendar.

Chapter 10

The Hanukkiah

The nine-branched candlestick used by the Jewish people for Hanukkah is called the *hanukkiah*. While its design is often similar to the biblical seven-branched menorah, it is distinct because of its nine branches. While the reasons for this emblem are perfectly clear to observant Jewish families, Christians are often confused because they do not find a nine-branched candlestick in their Scriptures.

The *hanukkiah* is used to commemorate the festival of Hanukkah, the feast of the dedication for which Jesus himself was present at the temple in John 10:22. (As a matter of fact, this is the only reference to Hanukkah in the canonical Scriptures). The nine flames of fire celebrate the great miracle that God manifested when his people rededicated the temple and reaffirmed their allegiance to the one God of their fathers.

The *hanukkiah* and the festival that it helps the Jewish

people commemorate originated in the time that Christian theologians often pejoratively call the "Intertestamental Period," the years between the last of the Minor Prophets and the beginning of the gospel era. While Christians have considered these the "silent years," the truth is that God was alive and well and that he was active among his people Israel.

Historical Desecration

In Hasmonean times, the city of Jerusalem and the Jewish people had fallen victim to a Hellenist zealot, Antiochus IV, the Seleucid king who styled himself Epiphanes (god manifest) but whom his subjects called Epimanes (madman). Antiochus first appeared at Jerusalem as a seeming deliverer, releasing the Jews from the power of the Ptolemys of Egypt. Within a short time, however, his passion to enforce the "civilization" of Hellenism upon all his subjects was directed at Judaea. Enlisting the support of some of the secularist and quasi-religious aristocracy of the biblical land, he stationed a garrison in Jerusalem and began an effort to syncretize Hellenism with the worship of God. When this was not received by the populace, he determined to force the Judaeans to accept Greek polytheism.

This policy escalated until the very temple sanctuary was desecrated when a statue of Zeus, the king of the Greek pantheon of gods, was erected in the Holy of Holies and the altar was defiled with the blood of a pig. Acts of sexual perversion and murder were also carried out in the sanctuary itself so that all of God's Ten Commandments were fully violated.

Finally, a contingent of guerrilla fighters, headed by Judah the Maccabee, succeeded in driving Antiochus from Jerusalem and Judaea. The evil despot ultimately died as Daniel 8:25 had predicted, "without hands," when he was consumed by a disease so horrible that his personal physicians could not bear to attend him.

When the Jews regained control of their temple, they found it polluted with pagan idolatry. Tradition suggests that even the temple menorah (the seven-branched lampstand) had been destroyed for its gold content. Obviously if the worship of God was to be reinstated, the temple had to be cleansed. And so it was. The priests and leaders went about the arduous task of removing all the polluted items and cleansing the sanctuary. According to tradition, a new menorah was constructed, perhaps even of inferior material to that which had once graced the holy place.

When the time came to light the temple menorah, the priests found that only one sealed vessel of oil, a one-day supply, remained from the devastation and pollution. The process of beating out olive oil and purifying it for temple use required seven days; therefore, the leaders were faced with a dilemma: should they light the menorah or wait for seven days? In their fervor for God, they decided to proceed immediately with the lighting of the menorah on *Kislev* 25, three years to the day after the desecration had occurred. The next day, to their astonishment, they found that the lights were still burning, and their amazement only grew as the light continued to burn for a total of eight days on that one day's supply of oil. This gave them the time to prepare additional consecrated oil that could be burned in the menorah. They recognized the miracle from God, signifying his approval of their rededication of his temple.

A FESTIVAL OF DEDICATION AND LIGHTS

From the first anniversary of the miracle forward, the Jewish people have observed the institution of a post-Torah festival called Hanukkah (Dedication). It was also known as the Festival of Lights, for it became a time for every Jewish family to light lamps on each of eight festival days until eight lamps burned together on the final day of the event. This observance commemorated the miracle of the oil and the light that burned for eight days. It was already an institution by the time of Jesus, as indicated by the reference in John 10. It was "winter," during the Jewish calendar's month of *Kislev*, when Jesus and his fellow Jews were present in Jerusalem for this festival.

From its beginning until the present day, Hanukkah has been a festival for celebrating one of the greatest historical challenges against Judaism–that of the subtle effort, not to destroy it, but to syncretize it with the polytheism of the ancient pagan world. All-out frontal attacks against Judaism's monotheism have been met with staunch resistance in which thousands of Jewish men, women, and children have given their lives as martyrs in order to "sanctify the name" of God. Antiochus' effort was initially more insidious and more dangerous to Judaism because it sought a blending Greek philosophy with Hebraic faith which, if adopted, would have destroyed Judaism from within.

Since Hanukkah commemorates victory over this attempt at syncretism, it has become a major Jewish festival around the world. When Jews engage in this family celebration during the eight days of Hanukkah, they realize that the survival of Judaism is dependent upon their own faithfulness to the Torah as the Word of God.

In Mishnaic times, the *hanukkiah* was to be positioned outside the entrance of the house to affirm publicly the Hanukkah miracle. It was to be placed on the left side of the door, with the *mezuzah* on the opposing right doorpost. It was thought that as a Jew passed through the door of his house during Hanukkah between these two sacred symbols, he fulfilled the biblical phrase in Song of Solomon 7:6: "How beautiful and how pleasant are you"–beautiful with the *mezuzah* and pleasant with the *hanukkiah*.

Originally, eight lamps or eight oil spouts were lit progressively during the festival; however, at some later time, a ninth branch or spout was added as a *shamash* or servant from which the other branches were lit. This is the reason that the *hanukkiah* today is a nine-branched candlestick, eight branches in honor of the miracle of light and one branch as a servant for lighting the others.

The *hanukkiah* has become one of the finest symbols of Judaism. Each year it is lit by Jewish families in the window of their homes to proclaim that God's faith is more powerful than darkness and that evil is overcome "not by might, nor by power" but by the Spirit of God.

CHRISTIANS AND HANUKKAH

Since Jesus himself was present at the temple for the Hanukkah celebration, it is certainly appropriate that Christians join with their Jewish brothers and sisters in commemorating the miracle that accompanied the rededication of the temple. It can serve as a time for Christians to reaffirm their commitment to the ethics of the Bible and to rededicate their lives and resources to the proposition that truth must be heralded around the world as the light that dispels darkness. It is a time to stand in solidarity with the international Jewish community, affirming that their religion will be defended with life and limb just as it was by the Maccabees and their followers. It is a season for remembering that the faith of the Bible must not be compromised with the syncretism of modern times and must stand as a distinct display of absolute ethics that calls all men to bow before the presence of the Almighty God and to observe his commandments.

Hanukkah is an excellent time for Christians to affirm the right of the Jewish people to self determination, free from political, economic, or religious coercion or intimidation, a right won on the ancient battlefield by the Maccabees. The church might use this occasion to remember its own Antiochus-like historical aberrations in forced baptisms, synagogue immolations, and general terror and mayhem against Jewish men, women, and children. And it might purpose that similar non-Christian actions will never again be perpetrated against Jews and Judaism.

LIGHTING THE LAMPS

Hanukkiot come in an endless variety of styles and sizes. Some are patterned after the temple menorah; however, most share only one common element: nine lamps. Christians can find one that suits their taste and then employ it during Hanukkah to light the lamps and thereby demonstrate both their solidarity with the international Jewish community and their determination to stand for the Light of God's Word.

The *hanukkiah* lamps are lit in the following manner: the *shamash* is used to kindle one lamp on the first evening of Hanukkah, two on the second, and so forth until all eight (plus the *shamash*) burn on the final night of the eight-day festival. The *hanukkiah* should be placed in or near a window on the front of the house to demonstrate to the world the importance of God's light.

Hanukkah, like Passover, is primarily a family celebration, a time for instructing children in the importance of dedication to God's Word. It can, however, be commemorated in a corporate setting in Christian congregations as a means of sharing with the Jewish community in their joyous celebration of victory over the insidious threat of assimilation and as a means of emphasizing the biblical truth so poignantly demonstrated in the miracle of the first Hanukkah, that dedication produces light.

The actual lighting of the candles (or lamps) of a *hanukkiah* is a powerful visual image that speaks more vividly than mere words. The dancing flames on the *hanukkiah* are living emblems, attesting to the power of God's light in men's lives.

Chapter 11

The Decalogue

The Decalogue (literally, the Ten Words or Utterances) is the Ten Commandments that God spoke to all of Israel (and, indeed, to all the world) at Sinai. The finest encapsulation of the absolute ethics of the One God of heaven and earth, the Decalogue is a symbol of monumental importance to the society of man. Every safe civilization is founded upon the principles espoused in these Ten Words. Without them, societies are lawless and encourage the manifestation of man's basest instincts.

In reality, all the commandments of the entire Bible are summed up in one word, the *Shema*: "Hear, O Israel, the Lord our God, is one Lord." This commandment enjoins the practice of monotheism upon God's people and requires them to love God with all their being. Jesus reaffirmed the primacy of this commandment and added another of the Torah's words as adjunct to it, "Thou shalt love thy neighbor as thyself." Then, he declared that all the Torah and the prophets (the entire Old Testament) were contingent upon these two commandments.

The Decalogue was divided into two tablets of five commandments each. On the one tablet were five commandments regarding man's relationship to God (including the requirement to honor his parents, the first of whom is God). On the other tablet were five commandments regarding man's relationship with his fellow man, If one were to observe the *Shema* fully, he would fulfill all ten of these words, for he would love God with all his being, and he would love his neighbor as himself.

All the other commandments of the Torah (603 in addition to the Ten Commandments) were subsets of one of these Ten Words, offering further detail of the ways in which one should go about fulfilling the Ten Commandments. This gives clarification to Paul's statement that all the law is fulfilled in this one word: *love* (Romans 13:9).

A SACRED SYMBOL

The Decalogue as a symbol is indeed a living emblem, because it visibly demonstrates the terms on which God first offered life and blessing to the fallen human race. Anywhere in the world where it is observed, it brings life and blessing, peace and tranquility. It is certainly proper that all believers in the God of the Bible display the symbol of his encapsulated will and Word. The Jewish people do not frequently display the Decalogue because in history the Christian church exalted the Ten Commandments to the exclusion of the remaining commandments. Though in the time of Jesus the Ten Commandments were accorded prominence in the Jewish community, subsequent rabbinic tradition made them equal to the rest of the 613 commandments.

Nowhere did Jesus or the apostles ever abrogate the commandments of God. If anything, Jesus strengthened the commandments by demonstrating that their violation began in the heart before it was manifest in the flesh. This truth is amply demonstrated in the so-called antitheses of the Sermon on the Mount. We are told repeatedly throughout the New Testament that those who violate God's commandments will not inherit the kingdom of God (Galatians 5:21). On the other hand, Jesus affirmed the fact that observance of the commandments would bring eternal life (Matthew 19:16-20).

The simple form of the Decalogue speaks loudly, trumpeting God's commandments as his continuing will for his people, both Jews and Christians, and all the world, for that matter. When one looks upon this form, he is reminded of the divine discourse at Sinai that formalized the words that would always be the manifestation of God's will for mankind.

Controversy has arisen in the United States and much of the western world over the public display of the Decalogue. Nations that were founded upon the principles set forth in the Ten Commandments now seek to ban their display in the city square. The Decalogue can no longer be displayed in public schools. Courts that adjudicate the law that was founded upon the Decalogue now refuse to display this symbol in their hallowed halls. One can only be reminded of the maxim of the Psalmist that the nation that forgets God will experience destruction (Psalm 19:17). Is it any wonder that prisons are crowded to overflowing and that schools have become places for violence? Is it any wonder that society is faced with a pandemic of AIDS and other sexually transmitted diseases?

TORAH SCROLLS

A more complete display of the Word and will of God is the Torah itself. Torah scrolls are visible emblems that bring to mind the ancient Word of God that is still alive and powerful. It is appropriate, therefore, for believers, both Jews and Christians, to possess Torah scrolls and to display them as a reminder of the foundation of their faith.

The Torah scroll in the synagogue is a most sacred symbol from which Jews can read, in the ancient language of their ancestors, the words of God. These scrolls are meticulously copied by hand by specially qualified scribes. They are handled with the utmost care and honor, for they are the very Word of God.

For Christians, though they recognize Jesus as the living Word of God, the Torah made flesh, there is still great significance in the scroll of the law. These symbols reinforce the fact that faith in God is not a new invention but an ancient tradition transmitted from generation to generation by the written Word of God that they contain.

Whether as a symbol or an actual scroll itself, this living emblem underscores the dependence of all believers upon the words of God for their very lives and sustenance. The living word contained in the scroll of the law is the light to man's pathway (Psalm 119:105) and a delight to those who follow the ways of the living God (Psalm 119:70).

LIVING EMBLEMS

The public and home display of the Decalogue serves as a reminder of God's code of ethics and is appropriate in every culture around the world. The very sight of the Ten Commandments is a powerful summons to biblical morality. Believers can make these living emblems clearly visible to their children so that they may understand that their lives are governed by much more than humanism's situational ethics. They are the children of God who follow his instructions implicitly because they love God and their fellow man.

Chapter 12

The
Star of David

For the secular and religious worlds alike, the Star of David has become the most universally recognizable symbol of modern Jews and Judaism. Formed by two interlocking equilateral triangles connecting the points of a hexagram, the Star of David is referred to in Hebrew as *Magen David* (the Shield of David). It can be constructed by intersecting the circumference of a circle with successive arcs the length of the circle's radius.

The Star of David is the focal point of the Israeli national flag and is used to mark the graves of Jewish soldiers around the world. In Israel, it is used to identify the public

relief agency that corresponds to the Red Cross: the Red Shield of David. Despite its popularity both in modern Judaism and in present-day secular societies, the Star of David's origin is not clearly biblical and remains a mystery.

FROM KING DAVID?

Because of its uncertain origins, the Star

of David has been the focus of much conjecture and speculation. Simply because of its name, it has been associated with King David. Rabbinic tradition asserts that when the *Amidah* (the first benediction of which praises God as the "Shield of Abraham") was prayed in David's time, the king asked God that another benediction be added praising God as the "Shield of David." David's request was rejected; however, such a reference was added to one of the lesser benedictions that concludes the *Haftarah* (reading from the Prophets).

Some have asserted that David actually used a shield featuring the interlocking triangle design when he fought Goliath. This, however, is a contradiction of the biblical text which emphasizes the fact that David carried only a staff, a shepherd's bag, and a sling. It could well have been possible that David used such a shield in his later battles; however, there is no solid evidence that such was the case.

It has been suggested that in later times in honor of King David, the Jewish people developed a shield that would identify their soldiers both to themselves and to their enemies (so that in the heat of hand-to-hand combat, one would not kill his own comrades). Since the *lingua franca* of that time was Greek, the way to honor King David and make his name the shield of the Jews was to use the Greek *delta* (which is an equilateral triangle) instead of the Hebrew *daleth* (d) in his name. The interlocking triangle was reflective of the double *daleth* of David's name, portrayed as superimposed double *deltas* (one inverted) in Greek. If this were the case, both the religious and secular worlds would have recognized the Shield of David displayed on the soldiers of Israel as a distinctively Jewish symbol, connected with Israel's most illustrious king.

A REACTION AGAINST PAGANISM?

It is possible that the origin of the Shield of David was a reaction against a pagan dualistic philosophy that threatened Judaism during the Babylonian captivity in the sixth century before the common era. The teachings of Zoroaster had spread from Persia throughout much of the known world of that time. Zoroastrianism's assertion that two equal powers ruled the universe was diametrically opposed to Judaism's strict monotheism. These two powers (or gods) were good and evil, manifest by light and darkness. Both powers were symbolized by a triangle, pointing either upward or downward, and men were required to choose which power they were to serve.

Even God himself addressed this dangerous affront to monotheism, the faith of the Jews. In Isaiah 45:5-8, he declared, "I *am* the Lord, and *there is* none else, *there is* no God beside me . . . I form the light, and create darkness: I make peace, and create evil: I the Lord do all these *things*." In the very time that Zoroastrianism was at its apex, God challenged the notion that there were two equal powers–good and evil–by declaring that he had created both good and evil, light and darkness.

It could well have been that in visible protest against this demonic teaching, Jewish leaders united the two separate Zoroastrian symbols into an even more powerful single emblem by superimposing the two triangles to form the Star of David as a symbol of the unity of God, the Master of both good and evil. How ironic it would have been if the People of the Book had co-opted the very emblems that challenged their faith and combined them to manifest the central truth of biblical religion!

A MESSIANIC SYMBOL

Because King David is so often recognized in Scripture and Jewish tradition as a messianic figure (one who prefigured the Messiah), it is quite natural that the *Magen David* would have significant messianic symbolism. One reason for such emphasis is the prophetic assertion by Balaam, the prophet for hire, that a "star" would arise from Jacob (Numbers 24:17). Perhaps this prophetic pronouncement originally applied to David; however, the sages of Israel interpreted it to be the Messiah. It was because of this tradition of identifying the Messiah with the Star of David that Bar Koziba called himself Bar Kochba ("Son of the Star") during the last Jewish rebellion against Rome in the second century C.E.

It is no coincidence that Jesus is called "the bright and morning star" in Revelation 22:16 and that he is called "the day star" in 2 Peter 1:19. The apostles of the earliest church clearly recognized in Jesus of Nazareth the Messiah of Israel (cf. Peter's declaration: "You are the Messiah, the Son of the living God," Matthew 16:16). They also applied the metaphor of "star" to their Master. Both Peter and John saw Jesus manifest physically with the surreal brightness of a star during his transfiguration (Matthew 17:2).

Indeed, Jesus is David's Star, the pristine light of the noonday. It is he who represented for the first and only time in history the union of God and man in one person, fully human and fully divine. He was the triune God reaching down to man, the triune being (body, soul, and spirit) that is reaching up to God. When the two were cojoined, there was a burst of light that then caused wise men to seek him and even now enlightens the heart of every man who calls upon his name.

PAGAN ORIGINS?

One of the great controversies regarding the Star of David is the fact that it has clearly been employed in various pagan and occult practices. As a matter of fact, historically the symbol was featured more extensively in heathen cultures than among the Jewish people. The possible pagan origin of the Star of David (or its expropriation and use in pagan traditions) even caused some Jews to abhor its use. Many Jews protested against the Star of David's display as a symbol of Zionism.

Numbers of Christians have also considered the Star of David's use to be associated with the world of the occult and have warned of its potential for evil. The hexagram, they say, is a Satanic symbol. There is, however, one major difference between the occult hexagram and the Star of David: the Star of David features two triangles that are interlocked, and the Star of David always stands on one point (not on two as with the occult hexagram).

Some have asserted that the *Magen David* is linked with the Druids who used the hexagram as a talisman against the drudes, the spirits of the night. Originally, they say, the star was the "shield of the Druid"; however, when the Jews were no longer interactive with the Druids, over time they shortened the Hebrew for Druid, *drvd*, to *dvd*, David's name. Because of the occultism inherent in the Celtic Druid tradition, the use of the Star of David has been proscribed by many.

For both Jews and Christians, the solution to the dilemma of what to keep and what to discard is stated well in Paul's advice, "Prove all things; hold fast that which is good" (1 Thessalonians 5:21). Simply because something has been the object of abuse is insufficient reason for discarding it. Even the most sacred of all names, Y/H/W/H, the very name of God himself, has been used in magical incantations in the occult world. If everything that has been corrupted were discarded, very little would remain.

Those Christians who would deprecate a symbol sacred to the Jewish people should also be aware that Christianity's symbol *par excellence*, the cross, is considered by many to have pagan origins. It is also abhorrent to the Jewish people whose ancestors were tortured and murdered under the sign of the cross. We must understand that virtually all symbols have been abused and polluted by Satanic influence at some point in time. Precluding their use on this ground is pusillanimous and ill advised.

HISTORICAL DOCUMENTATION

There is a relative paucity of historical evidence regarding the use of the Star of David as a symbol. The oldest undisputed example is from a seventh century B.C.E. seal belonging to one Joshua b. Asayahu. A Star of David can be seen at the second-century Capernaum synagogue in Israel. The use of the name *Star of David* can be traced only to the fourteenth century, where it was employed by David ben Judah the Pious. In 1354, King Charles IV commanded the Jews in Prague to use the "seal of David" on their ensign, "David's Flag." The Star of David has been more extensively employed by the Jewish people during the past two centuries.

CHRISTIANS AND THE STAR OF DAVID

Despite the controversy over the Star of David's possible origins in pagan traditions, it is a simple fact that no other symbol today identifies the Jewish people more clearly. Some have suggested that whatever its origin, the Star of David was sanctified by the Holocaust in which it was a compulsory badge on the clothing of the Jews and was often tattooed on the bodies of those in the death camps of the Nazi regime. It is certain that it speaks of the determination of upwards of six million martyrs to stand as God's chosen people even in the face of history's most vicious genocidal effort.

Because of the significance of the Star of David as a sign of Jewish identity, Christians should respect the symbol. Those who seek to reclaim Christianity's Jewish connection can rightly employ this symbol as they identify with both the ancient People of the Book and their living descendants. Because of the Star of David's messianic symbolism, Christians can see in it a symbol of their Jewish Lord.

Epilogue

It is not enough for Christians to be hearers and believers of the Word of God: they must be doers also. For far too long, the Christian church has been characterized by dogmatic faith, championing belief but failing to practice what it preaches. It has focused on orthodoxy when God is more concerned with orthopraxy. Jesus affirmed that what would cause the church to be the light of the world would be its "good works," not just its faith or its doctrinal beliefs, be they ever so sublime. The world will immediately recognize his disciples, taking note of those who have "been with Jesus," when it sees the manifestation of transcendent love that is shed abroad in the believers' hearts by the Holy Spirit, a love that completely fulfills all the Torah (Law of God) by imitating the life of Jesus in good works to "the least of his brethren."

"The word of God is alive and powerful." It is not a static, exhaustible resource. It is a living Word that brings renewal and fresh insight each time we examine it. By design, everything that is recorded in the pages of the Bible points to faith in the Messiah. The panorama of events, characters, and material objects manifest by God among his chosen people were symbols, similes, metaphors, allegories, and types and shadows of events, characters, and spiritual matters that were to be manifest in the life of Christ and the church.

The truth of this principle in no way diminishes the importance of what God did in pre-Christian times, nor does it minimize the value of what he continues to do with and among his chosen Jewish people to this day. It does, however, provide a foundation that validates the authenticity of what he has chosen to do among the Gentiles through the One who brought Israel's light to the nations.

Jesus is the new and living way who filled all the law and prophets full, adding depth and meaning to their predictive words by demonstrating what the Word made flesh would mean to the entire world: full and free salvation by grace through faith. He completed the faith of his Heavenly Father and of his earthly ancestors, validating its authenticity by providing an efficacious sacrifice that renewed and perfected the covenant and imbued it with eternal life.

THE "OLD TESTAMENT" AND JUDAISM

The faith of what the church has almost pejoratively called the "Old Testament" is not some antiquated, fossilized religion that should long ago have been buried in the sands of time along with other failed systems. The Jewish people are not legalists who should have been assimilated into the nations where they were dispersed never to be remembered again. Both the people and the book are chosen of God and are manifestations of his immutability and of his irrevocable covenants. Biblical Judaism was confirmed by supernatural, infallible witnesses to be God's system of praise, worship, and service. God cannot lie, and he cannot change. If Judaism were ever God's system of religion for mankind, in some form it must remain so. And so it is. Biblical Judaism produced many Judaisms at the beginning of the Common Era; however, only two survived, Rabbinic Judaism and Christianity, sister religions as it were. Authentic religious experience today is firmly rooted in the biblical Judaism through which Jesus and the apostles expressed their devotion to God.

The Word of God that the writer of Hebrews affirmed as "alive and powerful" is both the Hebrew Scriptures and the incarnate *Logos*. The "Old Testament" is the Bible from which Jesus and the apostles preached the gospel of the kingdom. It is the "God-breathed" Scripture that is profitable for teaching and instruction in righteousness so that believers may be mature and equipped for every good work. That is why it is so vital for the church to search the Scriptures, because what the Hebrew prophets, kings, and sages wrote as they were carried along by the Holy Spirit is that which testifies of Jesus and Christian faith, validating both for all time as the fullest expression of devotion to God.

GOD REVEALED IN MATERIAL THINGS

This is clearly true of the many material objects that God either designed himself or that his people constructed as manifestations of their obedience to his Word. They are, indeed, "living emblems," material symbols that take on life and meaning because of what they reveal. "For since the creation of the world [God's] invisible attributes, his eternal power and divine nature, have been clearly seen, being understood through what [he has] made, so that they are without excuse." Just as the universe bears witness to the existence and nature of its Maker, leaving men with no excuse for failing to seek, find, and obey the Eternal, so the material objects that God instructed his people to fashion are semaphores that call man to remembrance. Ever pointing the way to God, these emblems stand as guideposts that escort him past the treacherous precipices of life into the safety of life-giving relationship with his Maker.

While man's feeble attempts to fulfill the divine will do not always hit the mark and more often than not are flawed and imperfect, the attempt is what is important. Anyone who approaches God in simple faith he "will never drive away." When believers seek to do his will, he accepts the best they have to offer and gently leads them toward the more perfect day. Visible symbols of faith and remembrance bring them to the more excellent way of pure and total love that is manifest both to God and to man, thereby totally fulfilling the requirements of all God's commandments.

SYMBOLS OF FAITH

For the Jewish people, the *menorah*, the *tallit*, the *mezuzah*, and other objects that they have made in fulfillment of God's commands point the way in which they should walk (*halakhah*). These objects are constant, visual reminders that they are God's chosen people and that their chosenness makes them servants to him and to the world. They are living emblems that bespeak the life and vitality of God's Word and his covenants with his people.

These artifacts have become symbols of faith; therefore, they must be evaluated from an iconographic perspective if their ultimate meaning is to be understood. Their physical design helps establish their graphic history. Then, the graphic images are identified by the themes that are associated with them. This, in turn, reveals the symbolic value of these artifacts as icons that point beyond themselves to a greater reality by evoking the conception of that reality in the minds of the individuals who observe them.

WHY SYMBOLS?

Symbol and meaning establish man's world and create emotional safety in that world. In this context religious symbols would be of no intrinsic value if they did not generate emotions in the hearts of those who use them. The Roman poet Ovid observed that a symbol is "a form which means more than what is actually seen, an image of design with a significance . . . beyond its manifest content . . . an object or pattern which . . . causes effect in [men] beyond recognition of what is literally presented in the given form." Symbols, therefore, imply more than their mere appearance indicates. They have the capacity for generating emotional response in those who see them, thereby manifesting much more than their physical forms indicate. It is this emotional response to the image that gives longevity and enduring significance to the symbol itself. The "perennity of symbols, which survive their various and passing explanations, is conditioned by the perennity of man's condition."

The Jewish people are enriched by the artifacts that their history has produced. These living emblems ever point them to the God who has chosen them and gives them his light. Christians, too, can profit from these living emblems, recognizing them as authentic expressions of devotion to God and his commandments and as objects that have fulfilled their avowed purpose in pointing the way to God and to interaction with him. They point the way to Christ, expanding in their dynamic symbolism the meaning and depth of Christian faith, bringing richness and fulfillment to believers. What God has said works!

A RICH HERITAGE

This is especially true when Christians evaluate the richness of their heritage from the faith of Abraham manifest in the biblical Judaism of the Hebrew Scriptures. Both Paul and the writer of Hebrews declared that everything God commanded his people to do under the First Covenant foreshadowed realities that were to be manifest in the New Covenant, giving preview photographs as it were of the true and living Lord, the head of the church. What Israel did and does literally in remembrance of God, the church must do spiritually. As believers walk in the Spirit, the anointing that is in them by the gift of God's grace teaches them all things, helping them in the process of *imitatio Dei* by conforming them to the image of the living Christ. As believers walk with him in love, they discover the wonderful, affirming reality that "there is therefore no condemnation to those who are in Christ Jesus, who walk not according to the flesh, but according to the Spirit."

SENSORY PERCEPTION

Rather than being an attraction to sideline Christians in routine, repetitive ritual, these material Hebraic objects that God has inspired men to make from his written Word jog their memories and point them unfailingly to the living Word. They celebrate not the objects themselves but the Lord who is manifest in and through the principles that they reveal. The mature believer uses the object or symbol as a reminder, an aid to concentration on the invisible reality that the emblem represents.

Sensory perception was created by God himself. Men are impacted by what they see, what they hear, what they smell, what they touch, what they taste. Faith, therefore, is not some sublime mental exercise or even an attempt to detach oneself from both mind and body in some effort to contact the "god within," as monists do. Biblical faith is a living faith that involves every aspect of being–body, soul, and spirit. God must be worshipped with all the heart, soul, mind, and strength. Even meditation is a physical exercise in which the lips repeat the Word of God over and over (the meaning of the Hebrew words for "meditate day and night"[25]).

When believers interact with God, therefore, it is not just through subliminal meditation. They see God, they hear God, they taste God, they smell God, they touch God–not literally, but through the things that he has commanded or that they have devised to literalize their interaction with him. God is seen in visible symbols. He is heard in music and the spoken Word. God is tasted in the communion and in the table fellowship of the Christian meal that is shared with believers in any setting. They smell God in the rich aromas of the fragrant incense, the pungent anointing oil, and the smoldering candles. They touch God when they hold his Word in their hands, when they embrace "the least of his brethren."

LIVING SYMBOLS: A CALL TO FAITH

Emblems, then, are alive and powerful, for through them the Word of God is materialized, taking it from the abstraction of faith and manifesting it in the reality of good works that glorify the Father in heaven. Just as love is not love unless it proceeds from abstraction to action, so faith is not faith until its seed is brought to full flower in good works. Emblems are never ends in themselves. They must never become idols, objects of devotion, nor must they ever be totems or talismans by which one hopes to ward off evil. They must not be perceived as good-luck charms. God has specifically commanded that his people are not to make "any graven image" or to "bow down to them." Likewise, emblems should not be mere artifacts or eye-pleasing objects for the interior decorator.

Symbols should ever be billboards that grab men's attention in the maddening pace of the modern world, saying, "Stop, remember your Creator, make time for God." Modern man rushes headlong, often down precipitous paths, striving to fulfill ambitions, seeking for the satisfaction of self-actualization. They need someone to ring the bell, flash the lights, and drop the barricade to keep them from being consumed in self. God is that Someone, and the bells, lights, and barricades that he has erected are those symbols, emblems, and markers in time that he has specified in his Word.

For the Jew, the *tallit* is a daily reminder that he is to be enshrouded in the commandments of God, acknowledging his utter dependence upon God's grace and mercy. Every time he passes through the door of his home, touches the *mezuzah* that contains God's Word, and kisses his hand, he is reminded that El Shaddai is his protector. When he sees the menorah he receives a graphic vision of the light of life and of God's ever-watchful eye upon his people.

What rich lessons these and other living emblems teach Christians! They have the *tallit* of the Holy Spirit enshrouding them with God's Word. They have the blood of the Messiah applied to the *mezuzot* (doorposts) of their hearts. The New Covenant has engraved God's law on their hearts and in their minds by the *Shekhinah* of the Holy Spirit. The light of the Living Menorah illuminates their path. Because they have the living Christ within, they are well on their way toward being living emblems themselves, living "epistles," written and read of all men, witnesses to the saving grace of God through the good news of the risen Saviour, to whom be praise in the church both now and forever.

Index

Other Books by Dr. Garr

**God's Lamp
Man's Light:
Mysteries of the
Menorah**

**The Hem of
His Barment:
The Power in
God's Word**

**Bless You!
The Power of
the Biblical
Blessing**

**Our Lost Legacy:
Christianity's
Hebrew Heritage**

**Feminine & Free!
Restoring God's
Design for
Women**

**Christian
Celebrations
for
Passover**

**Jesus: When
God Became
Human**

**Church Dynamic:
Foundations
for Christian
Community**

**Family
Sanctuary:
The Biblically
Hebraic Home**

**Free at Last!
Releasing
Women for
Divine Destiny**

**Touching the
Hem: Jesus
and the
Prayer Shawl**

**The Book of
Blessings**

www.RestorationFoundation.org

HEBRAIC HERITAGE

CHRISTIAN CENTER

Hebraic Heritage Christian Center is an institution of higher education that is dedicated to the vision of restoring a Hebraic model for Christian education. A consortium of scholars, spiritual leaders, and business persons, the Center features a continually developing curriculum in which each course of study is firmly anchored in the Hebrew foundations of the Christian faith.

The Hebraic Heritage Christian Center vision combines both the ancient and the most modern in an educational program that conveys knowledge, understanding, and wisdom to a worldwide student population. The Center seeks to restore the foundations of original Christianity in order to equip its students with historically accurate, theologically sound understanding of the biblical faith that Jesus and the apostles instituted and practiced. At the same time the Center endeavors to implement the finest in innovative, cutting-edge technology in a distance-learning program that delivers its user-friendly courses by the Internet.

Among the wide range of services and products that Hebraic Heritage Christian Center offers are the publications of Hebraic Heritage Press. These are delivered both in traditional print media as well as in electronic media to serve both the Center's student population and the general public with inspiring and challenging materials that have been developed by the Center's team of scholars.

Those who are interested in sharing in the development of Hebraic Heritage Christian Center and its commitment to restoring the Jewish roots of the Christian faith are invited to join the Founders' Club, people who support this team of scholars and leaders by becoming co-founders of this institution. Many opportunities for endowments are also available to those who wish to create a lasting memorial to the cause of Christian renewal and Christian-Jewish rapprochement.

P. O. Box 450848 ✿ Atlanta, GA 31145-0848
www.hebraiccenter.org